SUFFICIENTLY ROBUST

SUFFICIENTLY ROBUST

Fifty Years of Walking in Grand Canyon

William Cathcart-Rake, M.D.

iUniverse, Inc.
New York   Bloomington

Sufficiently Robust
Fifty Years of Walking in Grand Canyon

iUniverse books may be ordered through booksellers or by contacting:

iUniverse
1663 Liberty Drive
Bloomington, IN 47403
www.iuniverse.com
1-800-Authors (1-800-288-4677)

ISBN: 978-1-4502-4501-2 (sc)
ISBN: 978-1-4502-4502-9 (ebook)
ISBN: 978-1-4502-4503-6 (dj)

Printed in the United States of America

iUniverse rev. date: 9/2/2010

For my wife Ruth and all those who have hiked with me
in the Canyon

Only by descending into the canyon may one arrive at anything like comprehension of its proportions, and the descent cannot be too urgently commended to every visitor who is sufficiently robust to bear a reasonable amount of fatigue.

—C.A. Higgins, "The Titan of Chasms,"
The Grand Canyon of Arizona, 1909

Contents

Acknowledgements

Friend and fellow Canyon hiker Chris Beck contributed two photographs for this book and allowed me to use several phrases from his song *Take Me Back* for the epigram in Chapter 18. Salina poet, novelist and writing instructor Patricia Traxler provided invaluable advice on presenting my memoirs. John Divine accompanied me on six of my Canyon treks. He made sure I returned to Grand Canyon at frequent intervals. Without his friendship, encouragement and support my story would be incomplete. Finally, I must thank my wife of nearly forty years who prompted me to record my memories, graciously allowed me to temporarily excuse myself from my duties as husband and parent to hike in Grand Canyon, and displayed extreme patience during the countless hours I spent preparing the manuscript.

Preface

Keep close to Nature's heart ... and break clear away, once in awhile, and climb a mountain or spend a week in the woods. Wash your spirit clean.

—John Muir (1838-1914)

In September 1996 I hiked in Grand Canyon for the ninth time. It was my sixth crossing of the Canyon via the main corridor trails. Prior to that hike, my wife Ruth urged me to keep a journal of my Canyon hikes. She also suggested that before my mental faculties totally failed, I should record memories of past experiences in Grand Canyon, imploring me to write it down and not just talk about it. Before leaving for the Grand Canyon in September 1996, I recorded memories of eight previous hikes, and I have kept a journal of all treks since then. I also have become a serious student of the Grand Canyon, learning more about its natural and human history and discovering what others have had to say about this place. The following is a formal narrative of my adventures in the Grand Canyon, a collection of my thoughts and experiences during nearly a half century of hiking in the Grand Canyon.

Although not a novice to hiking in the Grand Canyon, I am an enthusiast, not an expert. Most of my walks have been on trails accessible to hikers who are reasonably fit, possess a sense of direction and basic route finding ability, and exercise good judgment in their endeavors. This memoir is neither the musings of a naturalist nor intended to be a guidebook to hiking in the Grand Canyon, although I have referenced the U.S.G.S. quad map or maps for each of the trails I have hiked. For guidebooks to hiking in the Grand Canyon, I refer the reader to George Steck's *Hiking Grand Canyon Loops*, Harvey Butchart's classic *Grand Canyon Treks: 12,000 Miles Through the Grand Canyon*, Ron Adkison's *Hiking Grand Canyon National Park*, and Scott Thybony's *Official Guide to Hiking the Grand Canyon*. I also strongly suggest that anyone seriously interested in hiking in the Grand Canyon read *Over the Edge: Death in Grand Canyon*, by Michael Ghiglieri and Thomas Myers. The Grand Canyon can be a deadly place to hike, and the authors provide details of the deaths in the Grand Canyon as well as sage advice on how to decrease the chances of tragedy during a visit.

The Canyon is a long way from my home in Kansas. There are closer places to hike in beautiful surroundings, such as the prairie of my home state and the Rockies of neighboring Colorado. Nevertheless, I keep returning to Grand Canyon—despite the physical demands of the hike, despite the pain felt after the first day of hiking, despite the heat and dust. Does Grand Canyon hold some mystery I am trying to solve? Is there something I am trying to discover about myself or prove to myself by hiking in the Canyon? I suspect both questions can be answered in the affirmative. Grand Canyon is a special place to visit, and I am blessed that I can physically walk up and down the Canyon trails. I doubt that it would have the same attraction if I were unable to hike below the rim. Although neither exceptionally blessed with athletic talent nor inordinately obsessed with the Grand Canyon, I find myself mentally and physically invigorated spending time in this place—a place that never grows old for me. I cannot survey the Canyon from the rim without wanting to hike in it.

I see something new on each visit. Changes in weather, temperature, canyon wall colors, clouds, and hiking companions make each trip different, even when I am walking a route I have taken before. I relish the physical challenge and the spiritual renewal of the hike in this huge hole in the ground, whether it be a multi-day backpacking trip or a race across the Canyon in a day. Finally, I love sharing my appreciation of the Canyon with friends and family.

Chapter 1
First Crossing (Rim-to-Rim)

August 1961

Who can adequately describe the scene?—who can describe the indescribable?

In its stupendous ensemble the spectacle is too vast for art. It is indeed almost too much for human thought. You cannot behold it for the first time without a gasp, however blasé your emotions have become by globe-trotting.

—Fitz-James MacCarthy, "A Rhapsody,"
Grand Canyon of Arizona, 1909

I was a skinny kid, not at all athletic, content to ride my bike short distances, splash in the community pool, play catch with my brother, and begrudgingly mow our yard with a push lawnmower. I avoided walking long distances and running any distance. Given my lack of physical prowess, I was among the last chosen for a pickup game of baseball and the first cut after basketball tryouts. My father would occasionally take my brother Tim and me to the local golf course on Sunday afternoons. Dad would hit the ball around while his sons walked behind him. Walking the course with Dad was no treat for me. I wanted to ride in an electric cart.

1

In 1960, shortly after my eleventh birthday, I joined a Boy Scout troop in our sleepy little southern California town of Yorba Linda, the birthplace of Richard M. Nixon. This troop disbanded a year later, and my father encouraged me to continue with Scouts by joining Troop 99, the remaining troop in town. Every summer, Troop 99 spent five to six days hiking in either the Sierra Nevada Mountains of California or the Grand Canyon of Arizona. In August 1961, the troop planned a nearly twenty-five-mile hike across the Grand Canyon. Prior to joining Troop 99, I had not walked more than two miles in one day. What made me think walking nearly twenty-five miles in six days was possible? Was I overly optimistic about my physical abilities, stupid, or just naïve? Having neither been to the Grand Canyon nor seen a picture of it, it was a great unknown.

Boys who anticipated making the Grand Canyon trip were required to make at least two conditioning hikes with the troop during the months of June and July. These hikes always started at a building called "The Scout House," a small two-room structure near downtown Yorba Linda, which at the time was a small unincorporated Orange County village nestled amongst orange, lemon, and avocado groves. Yorba Linda's main drag, appropriately named Main Street, was one block long, and all of the town's commercial interests were located here. I can still picture the buildings lining the street: a hardware store, drug store, grocery store, weekly newspaper, five-and-dime, Masonic lodge, barbershop, beauty shop, bank, café, gift shop, gas station, Chevrolet car dealership, and Quaker church. The only other church in town, a Methodist church, was a block off Main. In the early 1960s there were no bars or liquor stores in town. The two local churches owned the sole liquor license. We had a volunteer fire department, usually called out to fight brush fires in the surrounding hills. Supposedly, a county sheriff patrolled the streets, although I never saw one. The town's children attended Yorba Linda Elementary School for kindergarten through eighth grade. After completing eighth grade we were bussed to high school in the neighboring community of Fullerton. Yorba Linda was the quintessential great place in which to be a kid.

A half dozen other boys and I made the two mandatory hikes, each time walking about five miles with packs on our backs, camping for the night, and hiking back the next day. Our routes led us beside and through the avocado and citrus groves and barley fields surrounding town. Rows of eucalyptus trees protected the fruit trees from high winds, their leaves emitting a characteristic fragrance that I will always associate with my boyhood home. The hikes in Yorba Linda were tough for me because they involved more walking than I had ever done, and an accursed pack had to be carried as well. Fortunately, these treks did not involve steep climbs or walking in extreme heat, and I discovered that I could walk five miles in one day.

Years later, I realized the training hikes did little to prepare me physically for a Grand Canyon hike. I suspect the scoutmaster determined which boys had the physical maturity and mental toughness to take on a bigger challenge. Somehow I managed to pass the test. One final preparation for the hike started two weeks prior to our departure. We had to repeatedly paint our feet with tincture of benzoin, supposedly to toughen the skin for the long walk. The stinky liquid only stained my feet brown.

Shortly after midnight one Saturday in August 1961, we started the journey from Southern California to the North Rim of Grand Canyon National Park, stopping for breakfast in Las Vegas, Nevada, and lunch at Zion National Park in southern Utah. My parents, my younger brother Tim, and my younger sisters, Marilyn and Jenny, accompanied nine hikers. Besides me, the Scouts were Kenny Quinn, Les Decker, Tom Dollarhide, Wendell Iwatsuru, and Torrey Webb. Our three leaders included Bob Ackerman, Jack McDavid, and Stan (last name long forgotten). A couple of Scouts rode with my family in our old Ford station wagon, while the remainder shared space with backpacks and other camping supplies in the back of a stock truck driven by the scoutmaster, undeniably an unsafe and uncomfortable mode of transportation.

Fitz-James MacCarthy, John Muir, and others have attempted to describe the nearly indescribable landscape one encounters upon peering over the Canyon rim for the first time. My first impressions of the Grand Canyon were its vastness, its wonderful array of colors, and the silence, broken only by a rush of wind from its depths. It was one immense gash in the earth. Additional adjectives could not adequately capture the scene. I had never seen a grander place in my life, but walking across it was another issue. The night before the hike I gazed across the Canyon, the lights of Grand Canyon Village on the South Rim twinkling in the distance, and a feeling of unease surfaced. How hard would it be to walk across this ten-mile-wide, mile-deep chasm?

After a day of sightseeing and acclimation on the North Rim, we started our 23.5-mile traverse across the Canyon. After depositing hikers at the trailhead, my mother drove our car to the South Rim, while my father drove the truck. Upon reaching the South Rim my father promised to make contact with a muleskinner and arrange for shipping extra supplies by mule train to Phantom Ranch at the bottom of the Canyon, where we would pick them up and use them for the second half of the hike.

Our leaders required that hikers wear long, light-weight, light-colored cotton pants (no stiff, heavy jeans), a long-sleeved white shirt, and a white pith helmet, attire designed to protect us from the intense summer sun. No markings identified us as Boy Scouts. My white shirt was a well-worn dress shirt handed down to me from my dad—a little large for me, but serviceable once I cut several inches off each sleeve. I must have brushed a half dozen coats of white enamel paint on my once khaki-colored pith helmet, the white layer meant to reflect the sun's harsh rays. Leaving the pith helmet its original khaki color was unacceptable, according to our leaders.

This trip predated specialized backpacking stores. The boys purchased gear from army surplus stores and searched through garages and attics for usable equipment issued to their fathers during stints in the military. My pack, heavy and incredibly primitive, was basically an eighteen-by-twenty-four-inch sheet of plywood with shoulder straps (made of two-inch-wide cotton webbing) attached to one side, with eyelet screws along the edges of the other side so that we could lash our gear, stuffed in a canvas bag, to the packboard. Troop 99 had an abundant supply of these instruments of torture. These packs did not feature padded shoulder straps, hip belts, modern fabric rucksacks, or space-age metal components. Additional gear consisted of an extra pair of socks, a six-foot-by-three-foot plastic sheet to be used as a poncho and ground cloth, a light blanket, a pair of moccasins for camp use, toiletries, a bowl and spoon, and a share of the cooking equipment and food. Given this relatively small load, my best friend, Les Decker, and I "buddy packed." We placed our gear in one bundle, strapped it to the packboard, and took turns carrying the load. While one of us toiled with the infernal pack, the other carried a canteen belt—an army issue web belt with four heavy steel one-quart canteens filled with water; two of the canteens nested in heavy steel canteen cups.

Les and I had few disagreements except when it came to Major League baseball. Having lived in New Jersey during his early childhood, Les followed his father's lead and became a New York Giants fan. Mr. Decker moved the family to Yorba Linda about the same time the Giants moved to San Francisco. Although transplanted to Southern California, home of my beloved Dodgers, Les remained a Giants fan. In response to hearing about the exploits of Willie Mays, Willie McCovey, and Juan Marichal, I sang the praises of my heroes, Sandy Koufax, Don Drysdale, Junior Gilliam, and Maury Wills. Our rivalry remained intense yet friendly, and we were a compatible team on the Canyon hike.

After saying good-bye to my family, the troop started down the North Kaibab Trail on a warm August morning. The North Kaibab Trail (U.S.G.S. maps: Bright Angel Point, Phantom Ranch) from the North Rim down Roaring Springs Canyon to Bright Angel Canyon was completed in 1927 to replace the original route to Bright Angel Canyon—the Old Bright Angel Trail—located several miles to the northeast. The Old Bright Angel Trail followed a route used by the Indians and prospectors and was improved in 1902 by Francois Matthes, a U.S.G.S. geologist and mapmaker. The newer North Kaibab trailhead was much closer to the visitor facilities on the North Rim than the Old Bright Angel Trail.

During our descent of the North Kaibab Trail we periodically encountered mule trains carrying visitors up and down the trail. The muleskinner barked out orders for us to move to the uphill side (inside edge) of the trail and remain silent until all mules had passed. For a brief moment I felt morally superior to the mule riders. I was the purist—walking my way across the Grand Canyon, while they were riding a short distance into the canyon on a stinking mule. However, it would have taken very little encouragement for me to hop on that mule and ride the rest of the way to our destination.

Summer months are undeniably the worst months to hike in the Canyon because of the searing summer heat in the inner canyon. Daytime high temperatures regularly exceed one hundred degrees during June, July, and August, and nighttime lows rarely fall below seventy degrees. Unfortunately, because of our school schedule, summer was the only time we could make a weeklong trip. Our leaders were aware of the weather in the Canyon in August, and they made sure we carried plenty of water, rested frequently, and avoided uphill walks in the heat of the day.

The temperature rose as we descended the many switchbacks through the upper layers of the Canyon. My thighs burned from the steep downhill walk. This walk was nothing like those I had taken in Yorba Linda.

The thin straps of my pack cut into my shoulders. I swore they were made of barbed wire. Trading the pack for the canteen belt lessened the load on my back but brought no reprieve from the heat. Rest stops did not occur often enough for me. So this was what descending into hell was like. I shuffled my feet down the dusty, winding trail—kicking up red dust in the Hermit Shale, Supai Formation, and Redwall. More than one of the hikers behind me cried out, "Pick up your feet."

"Eat my dust," I wanted to reply.

The trail cut through the Redwall on the south side of Roaring Springs Canyon. Across the gorge water poured out of the rock wall and cascaded to the canyon floor on its way to join Bright Angel Creek and eventually the Colorado River. A lush hanging garden clung to the wall surrounding the springs. The creek formed by Roaring Springs was the largest tributary of Bright Angel Creek.

Below the Redwall the dust I generated from my shuffling gait became brown. Not far from Roaring Springs, the trail intersected Bright Angel Canyon and turned south, following a nearly straight line beside Bright Angel Creek to the Colorado River eight miles downstream. Once out of the confines of Roaring Springs Canyon we could see our final destination, the South Rim, on the far southern horizon. It appeared a long distance away.

As we walked along Bright Angel Creek I silently wished our scoutmasters would stop and let us cool off in one of the many clear, natural pools in the creek—some large enough to accommodate our entire group. Only upon reaching our first night's campsite in late afternoon were we finally allowed to soak in the chilly waters of the stream. There were no improvements at this camp—just a wide spot in the trail on the west bank of the creek, approximately seven miles from our starting point and seven miles upstream from the Colorado River. I have no idea whether our campsite was near Cottonwood Campground, which was located on the east bank of Bright Angel Creek one mile below Roaring Springs Canyon.

Cottonwood Camp was established in the 1920s as a layover for mule riders on their way to the Colorado River from the North Rim. In the 1930s, the Civilian Conservation Corps improved the campground. I cannot remember seeing Cottonwood Camp on the walk. Focused on keeping up with the boy ahead of me, observing the scenery was low priority.

The boys on the trip were divided into three groups: Ackerman's Aces (led by Scoutmaster Bob Ackerman), Mac's Maniacs (led by Assistant Scoutmaster Jack McDavid), and Stanley's Steamers (led by Stan, a college student and assistant Scout leader). Each group was assigned daily tasks. One group gathered wood for the fire and washed dishes, the second group cooked, and the third enjoyed a day off. We rotated duties daily. Les and I were assigned to Bob Ackerman's group. Mr. Ackerman was strict, quick to criticize our shortcomings, and demanded obedience. The boys called him Mr. Ackerman. Raised to respect my elders, I listened to him and generally followed his commands. In contrast, Les disliked Mr. Ackerman's dictatorial style and repeatedly, and unsuccessfully, challenged his authority. Mr. Ackerman kindly reminded Les that the scoutmaster would determine when and how tasks would be done on this trip.

Short, thin, and prematurely grey, Mr. McDavid led by example rather than fiat. Mr. McDavid could be stern, but he was kind. He loved the hike and related well to the kids—a leader, yet one of the guys. To me, he was Jack or Mac, not Mr. McDavid. Jack had been a medic in the Marine Corps in the Pacific Theater in World War II, but he chose not to dwell on the horrors he had witnessed. I never heard him tell a war story. At each rest stop Jack enjoyed a Pall Mall cigarette, teaching us how to field strip a cigarette in case we took up the smoking habit. He also taught us how to apply moleskin to hotspots on the skin of our feet to prevent blisters. Jack shared our sentiments about the heat and complained that his pack was just as heavy and his legs were just as tired as ours. The boys made sure his pack was heavier (when it was unguarded, we would sneak a few rocks into his pack).

In 1961, wood fires were allowed in the Canyon, so we cooked directly over wood coals. Food was memorable for how bad it was. Our meals consisted primarily of first-generation dehydrated products such as Chili Mac, a dreadful mixture of macaroni and highly seasoned chili. Additional foodstuffs included beef stew, dried beef, cheese, oatmeal, stewed prunes, Hershey tropical chocolate bars, hard, thick crackers called pilot biscuits, and powdered eggs. Pilot biscuits were nothing more than thick, petrified saltine crackers made a little more palatable by smearing them with the jelly and peanut butter, each magically made by mixing water with a bag of dehydrated ingredients. The tropical chocolate bars were as tough as a bar of soap, although a bit tastier. I hated eggs as a kid and the powdered eggs in camp were an order of magnitude worse than the eggs my mother made me choke down for breakfast at home.

On the trail we were periodically issued lemon drops to moisten our mouths. We obtained water from the stream and drank or used it for cooking without any treatment. Our scoutmaster reassured us that any contaminants that found their way into the stream water were eliminated by the turbulent flow of the stream and the exposure to the sun and air—a myth I believed for years.

We camped beneath the stars, sleeping under light blankets on plastic ground cloths spread on a flat spot. Neither air mattresses nor camping pads cushioned our aching bodies on the hard, uneven earth. No matter how hard I tried to clear the earth under my ground cloth of sticks and stones, something inevitably poked me in the back or side. Fatigue overcame discomfort, and sleep overtook me. We kept mosquitoes at bay with insect repellant. I had no idea that rattlesnakes and scorpions inhabited the Canyon and that their bites could cause more misery than a mosquito's.

At first light of our second day, the crackling of the campfire awakened me. Everyone groused about his stiff joints and sore muscles. I had dishwashing duty after breakfast and somehow managed to lose grasp of a large cook pot I was rinsing in the rushing water of Bright Angel Creek. I frantically cried out, "What do I do, what do I do?" Mr. Ackerman barked, "Get the pot!" My buddies howled with laughter at my predicament. I chased downstream in pursuit of the pot floating on the rushing water, worried about the punishment in store if I returned empty-handed and embarrassed that I had created such a scene. Fortunately, the pot filled with water and sank in a deep pool not far from camp. Relieved but humiliated, I stripped to my undershorts and waded into the cold water to retrieve the errant pot.

Following our overnight stop in upper Bright Angel Canyon, we started the seven-mile walk to Bright Angel Campground on the west bank of Bright Angel Creek near its confluence with the Colorado River. My legs were grateful that this segment was relatively flat and not the knee-jarring downhill walk of the previous day. Approximately one mile below our first camp, we passed Ribbon Falls on our right, located in a small side canyon on the west side of Bright Angel Creek. Ribbon Falls was reached by taking a spur trail off the main corridor trail, crossing Bright Angel Creek by a footbridge, and walking a short distance west. A side trip to Ribbon Falls was not on our itinerary. I did not particularly want to take the extra steps to get there anyway. My eyes remained focused on the feet of the boy ahead of me, moving my feet when his moved, stopping when he stopped. Lizards silently scurried across the trail, seemingly daring me to try and step on him or her. They were far too quick for my tired legs to pounce upon.

After several more miles of hiking we entered The Box—a severe narrowing of Bright Angel Canyon. A scoutmaster informed us that the canyon walls through which we walked were among the oldest exposed rocks in the world. I wasn't impressed with the age of the rocks, but I was impressed with the narrow alley through which we walked—the trail and Bright Angel Creek sandwiched between two vertical walls of black and pink rock.

About a half mile upstream from Bright Angel Campground, the canyon widened and we passed through Phantom Ranch, a fourteen-acre tourist camp. Phantom Ranch was built in 1922 by the Fred Harvey Company, which had acquired a tent camp established in 1903 by David Rust. Rust's Camp was renamed Roosevelt Camp in 1913 after Theodore Roosevelt's visit to the site. In 1922 the Fred Harvey Company changed the name to Phantom Ranch after Phantom Creek, a tributary of Bright Angel Creek located approximately one mile above Phantom Ranch.

The Fred Harvey Company operated all hotels and restaurants along the Santa Fe Railroad lines, and Grand Canyon was a featured destination in the Southwest, especially after completion in 1901 of a spur from the mainline at Williams, Arizona, to the South Rim. It was only natural for the Fred Harvey Company to expand its domain into the bottom of the Grand Canyon. Visitors could stay in Fred Harvey accommodations on the South Rim, ride Fred Harvey mules to the bottom of the canyon, and stay at Fred Harvey's Phantom Ranch.

Mary Colter (1869–1958), an architect and interior designer working for the Fred Harvey Company, designed Phantom Ranch, which consisted of more than a dozen rustic stone and wood buildings scattered through the cottonwoods along Bright Angel Creek. Mary Colter designed many other buildings in Grand Canyon National Park, including Indian Watchtower at Desert View, and Hopi House, Lookout Studio, and Bright Angel Lodge in Grand Canyon Village on the South Rim. Her structures typically blended with the natural surroundings.

Phantom Ranch provided meals and overnight lodging for mule riders and hikers who preferred meals in a dining hall and a bed in a cabin to camping at nearby Bright Angel Campground. Phantom Ranch also featured a swimming pool built by the Civilian Conservation Corps in the 1930s. Bright Angel Creek fed the pool. The pool was demolished and covered over in 1972 because of difficulties meeting health standards.

The heat at Bright Angel Campground in the inner canyon was oppressive, even in the shade of the many cottonwoods growing along the banks of the creek. The ancient black rock walls of Vishnu Schist (1.8 billion years old) absorbed the heat during the day and radiated it back at night. Sleeping in the furnace-like conditions proved difficult.

Our troop spent two and a half days at Bright Angel Campground, an improved facility featuring running water and flush toilets. Much of our time was spent trying to keep cool by sitting in the shade or soaking in the chilly waters of Bright Angel Creek. One day we swam in the pool at Phantom Ranch. Another day Les Decker, Bob Ackerman, and I walked up Bright Angel Creek above Phantom Ranch to fish. Our fishing equipment consisted of a store-bought fly tied on a piece of fishing line attached to a branch found along the creek. There were trout in the stream, but they eluded our angling attempts.

While Les and I fished, the rest of the troop hiked a couple of miles up Clear Creek Trail (U.S.G.S. map: Phantom Ranch), which started 0.3 mile north of Phantom Ranch. The Civilian Conservation Corps built Clear Creek Trail in the 1930s as a route to reach Clear Creek to the east. A hike to Clear Creek involved an ascent to the Tonto Plateau, where the trail remained for most of its 8.7-mile length. The trail coursed east above the Colorado River and then northeast above Clear Creek before descending to the stream. While at Bright Angel Campground we also took delivery of additional supplies from a mule train from the South Rim—my father had successfully completed his mission. We would have food for the climb out!

Awakening at midnight on the fifth day of our trek, we began our ascent out of the Canyon. We planned to hike from the Colorado River to Indian Garden, an oasis along Garden Creek on the Tonto Plateau, during the relatively cooler hours of the night and by the light of a full moon. Our scoutmaster forbade using flashlights during the night hike. He told us that our eyes would adjust to the dark; like nocturnal animals, we would have no problem following the trail.

We crossed the Kaibab Suspension Bridge to the River Trail on the south bank of the Colorado River (U.S.G.S. map: Phantom Ranch). The Kaibab Suspension Bridge across the Colorado River (also known as the Black Bridge) was erected in 1928 to replace a cable with suspended cage constructed by David Rust in 1907 to link the North and South Rims. The cage was large enough to hold a man and a mule and was pulled back and forth from one side of the river to the other. The Kaibab Bridge connecting the North and South Kaibab Trails measured four hundred forty feet long and lay seventy-eight feet above the Colorado River at low water. Eight main cables supported the bridge, each five hundred fifty feet long and weighing 2,320 pounds. The cables could not be loaded on mules; forty-two Havasupai Indians spaced at ten- to twelve-feet intervals carried each cable 6.4 miles down the trail to the construction site. The bridge can carry the weight of a string of loaded pack mules.

Completed in 1936 by the Civilian Conservation Corps, the River Trail was blasted out of the 1,700-feet high cliffs of the Vishnu Complex of the Inner Gorge to link the South Kaibab and Bright Angel Trails. Prior to the completion of the River Trail, hikers and mule riders had to travel a four-mile stretch of the Tonto Trail between Indian Garden and the South Kaibab Trail to reach Phantom Ranch. The nearly two-mile-long River Trail coursed along the south side of the Colorado River from forty to five hundred feet above the high water mark. The trail engineers planned to change the name of the trail to memorialize the first worker killed during its construction. Although several workers were injured, none died, and the trail retained its original name.

We followed the River Trail a short distance on a night as dark as a pocket. Below us the Colorado River could be heard but not seen. Cloud cover obscured the promised full moon. Jack slowly led us on the darkened path without aid of moonlight or flashlight. Although I did not witness the event, rumor has it that Jack nearly walked off the trail carved into the cliff high above the river—narrowly avoiding serious injury or death. Fortunately, a couple of companions grabbed him before he plunged to the river below. Jack wisely called a halt to forward progress. So much for a midnight hike.

We sat on the dusty trail and waited for daybreak. When visibility improved, we proceeded along the River Trail to the foot of Bright Angel Trail at Pipe Creek and climbed out of the inner gorge, completing the nearly five-mile walk from Bright Angel Campground to Indian Garden before the sun started to bake the Tonto Plateau.

The Bright Angel Trail (U.S.G.S. maps: Grand Canyon, Phantom Ranch) followed a natural break in the cliffs formed by the massive Bright Angel Fault. It was originally used by the Havasupai Indians to travel between the South Rim and Indian Garden, where they grew corn, beans, and squash along Garden Creek. Prospectors Ralph and Niles Cameron and Pete Berry laid claim to the area and improved the trail in 1890. Ralph Cameron eventually bought out his partners and took control of the trail. In 1902 he extended the trail from Indian Garden to the Colorado River. Because Cameron held more than 13,000 acres in mining claims along the Bright Angel Trail, he could control access to the trail and designated it a toll road. From 1903 until 1924, Cameron charged travelers down the Bright Angel Trail a one-dollar toll. He profited more from tourists than mining. After years of bitter wrangling with the cantankerous Ralph Cameron, the National Park Service took ownership of the trail in 1928 and the few Havasupai Indians still farming at Indian Garden were chased out. The rights of visitors to the park superseded the practices of generations of Native American canyon dwellers.

At Indian Garden we found refuge in the shade of cottonwoods planted by Ralph Cameron in the early 1900s. Later that afternoon we walked out to Plateau Point to view the Colorado River, nearly 1,300 vertical feet below, and to watch the sunset over the canyon. Someone accidentally knocked Torrey Webb's pith helmet off his head, and it sailed over the guardrail at Plateau Point and out of sight—presumably floating to the river below. Torrey was forced to wear Mr. Ackerman's helmet the remainder of the trip, lest he appear different from the rest of the boys.

We left Indian Garden by mid-morning of day six for the 4.6-mile climb from Indian Garden to Grand Canyon Village on the South Rim. The ascent out of the Canyon was just as tough as the descent had been several days earlier. When the trail direction reversed at one of multiple switchbacks leading to the rim, a hiker at the end of the line would cry out to Jack McDavid at the front of the line, "You're going the wrong way." This attempt at humor quickly became tiresome. The uphill grade and the more than mile-high elevation had me gasping for breath. The pungent odor of mule urine fermenting in large puddles along the trail had me holding my breath. The climb out seemed interminable, but by mid-afternoon we reached the rim. I remember the deep satisfaction of completing the rugged hike—at least rugged for a scrawny twelve-year-old kid. To that point in my life, it was the hardest physical challenge I had faced.

From the South Rim I could see across the wide gorge to the opposite side. The Canyon looked every bit as wide from this vantage point, but now I knew I was capable of walking across it. Red dust permanently stained my white socks and white shirt, and the Grand Canyon left an indelible impression on me. Despite the heat, the hard work of the hike, bad food, my uncomfortable pack, and sleeping on hard ground, I wanted to return and hike in the Canyon. The seeds of my love affair with Grand Canyon were planted. What was it about this place? It would be many years and many miles of hiking in the Canyon before I would even begin to offer an explanation.

View from South Rim towards Bright Angel Canyon

Chapter 2
Havasu

June 1966

After graduation from Fullerton Union High School in June 1966, I returned to Grand Canyon with Boy Scout Troop 99. This was to be my last hike with the troop, as I left Yorba Linda later that summer for the University of Colorado in Boulder, and shortly thereafter my parents moved the family from the land of milk and honey to Dorothy's home state of Kansas. Originally the troop planned to repeat the trip of five years earlier (North Rim to South Rim crossing), but heavy spring rains flooded Bright Angel Canyon, destroying portions of the North Kaibab Trail and five of the seven footbridges between rim and river, and disrupting completion of a new pipeline started in 1965 to deliver water from Roaring Springs to the South Rim. The original water supply from Indian Garden was no longer adequate to meet the needs of the burgeoning tourist invasion. A cross-canyon trek impossible, we settled for a hike into Havasu Canyon (outside the national park boundaries), a major side canyon in the western part of Grand Canyon.

The Havasupai (people-of-the-blue-green-water), one of the smallest Native American tribes in the United States, has inhabited Havasu Canyon since A. D. 1300. The Havasupai Indian Reservation, which bordered the national park, was the home to the only Native American tribe living in Grand Canyon. The Havasupai considered themselves the traditional guardians of the Grand Canyon. In 1966, fewer than three hundred Indians lived in Supai Village and environs, a reservation of five hundred eighteen acres on the canyon floor, eight miles by foot or horseback from the rim.

Prior to the establishment of the reservation in 1881, the Havasupai spent the winter months on the plateau above the canyon where firewood and game were plentiful and returned to their canyon home in spring to raise crops. On arable land along Havasu Creek they grew corn, melons, beans, squash, and pumpkins, and maintained a few fruit trees. After 1881, the Havasupai were restricted to their tiny reservation on the canyon floor. At the time of our visit in 1966, the Havasupai still farmed their small plots in Havasu Canyon, but tourism had become a significant source of income. Not until 1975 did the federal government return 531,000 acres of traditional homeland on the plateau above Havasu Canyon to the tribe—increasing the size of the Havasupai reservation a thousand-fold.

We bussed from Yorba Linda to the trailhead on Hualapai Hilltop at 5,200 feet in elevation. Hualapai Hilltop is approximately sixty-eight miles north of Peach Springs, Arizona, and one hundred ninety-three road miles from Grand Canyon Village. Our final destination was a campground approximately 2,000 vertical feet below and ten miles from Hualapai Hilltop (U.S.G.S. maps: Supai, Havasu Falls). The western Grand Canyon is not as deep as that traversed by the main corridor trails from North Rim to South Rim. In my opinion, the vista from Hualapai Hilltop did not rival the views from Bright Angel Point on the North Rim or from multiple vantage points along the South Rim near Grand Canyon Village. Our visual reward lay hidden in the depths of the Canyon along Havasu Creek.

The hike to Havasu Canyon was considerably easier for me than my hike in the Canyon in 1961. Although we hiked the entire ten-mile distance to the campground in one day, the descent was not as steep and the vertical drop was less than half that encountered on my first hike. Heat presented the main obstacle this trip, as inner canyon temperatures exceeded one hundred degrees during the day in late June.

During the five years since my first Canyon trek, I had hiked countless miles with Troop 99 in various locations in California, including Yosemite and Sequoia National Parks. I also started competitive swimming as a sophomore in high school, and undoubtedly this contributed to my improved physical condition—still skinny, still uncoordinated, but stronger and capable of carrying heavier loads. In a show of physical prowess—or was it just showing off?—I packed a watermelon on a short hike near Yorba Linda. On another trip I carried a cast iron Dutch oven in which I later cooked a pot roast and peach cobbler.

An early-generation aluminum pack frame with canvas rucksack replaced the packboard of my last Canyon trip. The new pack frame featured padded shoulder straps that did not cut into my shoulders, a big improvement over the thin, unpadded straps on the packboard I used in 1961. However, I coveted the pack carried by another Scout—a Kelty brand external-frame pack with padded shoulder straps, a hip belt, and a lightweight nylon compartmentalized pack sack with side pockets. At the time I believed that Kelty produced the best backpack in the world. I wondered if I would ever be able to afford such luxury, as my parents refused to indulge me with such a purchase.

Instead of sleeping directly on the hard ground, I had a plastic air mattress that provided a modicum of comfort and could be used to float on Havasu Creek. Leaving nothing to chance, I carried two air mattresses in case one of them developed a leak.

In contrast to the small group hiking the Canyon in 1961, thirty-four boys, including my brother Tim, and five adult leaders snaked their way down the trail to the canyon floor. Jack McDavid, now the scoutmaster, set the pace, his self-assigned task for every hike I made with him from 1961 until 1966. Jack was a master at leading a walk. His cadence was as steady as a metronome and slow enough that the weakest hikers could stay with him.

The Havasu Trail crossed the Havasupai Indian Reservation and intercepted Havasu Creek 6.5 miles from Hualapai Hilltop. The trail continued beside Havasu Creek to Supai Village, where the tribe assessed a trail usage fee. We saw few villagers as we marched through town. Jack McDavid pointed out the two red rock pillars overlooking the village. These stone monoliths, called *Wigleeva*, are the guardian spirits of the Havasupai tribe. According to Havasupai legend, if the *Wigleeva* ever fall, the canyon walls will close and destroy the people.

We walked two miles beyond Supai Village to Havasu Campground (elevation 3,030 feet). The campground stretched along the banks of

Havasu Creek between Havasu and Mooney Falls. Besides our group, only a handful of other hikers camped under the cottonwoods just beyond one-hundred-twenty-foot-high Havasu Falls. Trusting that the weather would stay warm and dry, our troop left tents at home, preferring to sleep exposed to the heavens.

The blue-green water of Havasu Creek and its travertine pools were inviting after the ten-mile hike. Lush vegetation grew along the banks of the stream. The turquoise hue of Havasu Creek, the result of the blue sky reflecting off the white creek bed created by sediment of calcium sulfate, magnesium carbonate, and calcium carbonate, added to the tropical affect. The chilly creek water was refreshing after a long walk in the furnace-like conditions of the canyon. We discovered that we could climb behind Havasu Falls and jump through the falls into a deep pool at the base of the falls.

The troop spent four days in Havasu Canyon, settling into a routine of sleeping from dusk to dawn, packing away our sleeping bags after awakening lest they become homes to wandering scorpions, preparing breakfast, cleaning up, soaking in the creek, preparing lunch, cleaning up, soaking in the creek, preparing dinner, cleaning up, and rolling out ground clothes, sleeping pads, and bags in preparation for the night. We depended upon lightweight dehydrated foods for the major portion of our diet and cooked over wood or charcoal fires. Troop members were divided into three groups who daily rotated the chores of cooking, gathering firewood, and washing dishes. One morning we explored one-hundred-ninety-foot Mooney Falls a mile downstream from our campsite. Mooney Falls was named after Daniel Mooney, an Irish prospector who allegedly fell to his death trying to descend the cliff beside the falls to the base on a one-hundred-fifty-foot rope. He failed to account for the remaining forty feet to the bottom.

The older Scouts, including me, and a couple of leaders took a 6.3-mile side trip down Havasu Creek to the Colorado River. The trail to the river was poorly defined and crossed Havasu Creek multiple times. Ankle high hiking boots, mandatory for all hikes with Troop 99, were left in camp. Not wanting to ruin leather boots wading in the water, we wore old tennis shoes for the jaunt down the creek. When we couldn't find a trail, we simply walked in the creek, plopping into one of many pools along the way when the heat became unbearable.

Our small group spent the night near the junction of Havasu Creek and the Colorado River (156.7 miles downriver from Lee's Ferry). The assistant scoutmaster responsible for packing food for this trip miscalculated the caloric needs of a ravenous group of teenagers—half rations for dinner and breakfast had to suffice. Hungry and tired, we returned to our base camp near Havasu Falls the next morning, where Jack McDavid immediately cooked a second breakfast for us.

The following day the troop hiked out of the canyon, completing most of the mileage to Hualapai Hilltop in the cool evening hours. I appreciated the beauty of the western Grand Canyon, especially along Havasu Creek, but preferred the landscape of my first trip—the steep cliffs, the mile deep canyon, the endless landscape of temples and buttes, and the narrow side canyons through which we walked. I longed for the Canyon I had hiked in five years earlier.

Chapter 3
Rim-to-Rim-to-Rim

May 1974

According to Major Powell, it is about two hundred and seventeen miles long, from five to fifteen miles wide from rim to rim, and from five thousand to six thousand feet deep. So tremendous a chasm would be one of the world's greatest wonders even if, like ordinary canyons cut in sedimentary rocks, it were empty and its walls were simple. But instead of being plain, the walls are so deeply and elaborately carved into all sorts of recesses—alcoves, cirques, amphitheaters, and side canyons—that were you to trace the rim closely around on both sides your journey would be nearly a thousand miles long.

—John Muir, "Our Grand Canyon," 1902

John Muir was born in Scotland in 1838 and emigrated to the United States with his family in 1849. At the age of twenty-two Muir enrolled at the University of Wisconsin–Madison but left several years later without graduating. He worked as an industrial engineer in Indianapolis in 1866 and 1867 before enrolling in what he called the "university of the wilderness," walking a thousand miles from Indiana to Florida. Muir migrated to San Francisco in 1868 and soon thereafter visited Yosemite for the first time. He became a champion of the natural wonders of Yosemite Valley in California. In 1892 John Muir wrote to the editor of *The Century Magazine*, a popular monthly magazine published from 1881 until 1930, "Let us do something to make the mountains glad." Shortly thereafter Muir helped found the Sierra Club and served as its first president until his death twenty-two years later on Christmas Eve 1914.

In 1903, John Muir and President Theodore Roosevelt traveled together to Yosemite Valley. During that trip Muir convinced Roosevelt that federal control and management were necessary to protect the valley. Muir, a patron saint of the environmental movement, was concerned with the protection of Nature for the spiritual advancement of humans and for Nature itself. He preached on the inseparable connection between man and the rest of creation, claiming "when we try to pick out anything by itself, we find it hitched to everything else in the universe."

John Muir visited Grand Canyon many times, and in an 1898 issue of the *Atlantic Monthly,* he wrote, "So incomparably lovely and grand and supreme it is above all the canyons in our fire-molded, earthquake-shaken, rain-washed, wave-washed, river and glacier sculpted world." He ended his article by urging its establishment as a national park. It would take another twenty-one years for Muir's wish to come true.

Grand Canyon National Park includes over a million acres of land—1,218,375.54 acres, to be exact. In river miles it is two hundred seventy-seven miles long, starting at Lee's Ferry (river mile 0) upstream and ending at the Grand Wash Cliffs (river mile 277). In air miles it is one hundred ninety miles long. The width of Grand Canyon varies from less than a mile to 17.5 miles rim to rim. At its deepest, it is 6,000 vertical feet from rim to river. There are four hundred miles of trails in the Canyon and only 30.7 are regularly maintained—the main corridor trails. Over five million people visit the national park every year and only one percent of them hike the trails below the rim. Most of the visitors are content with briefly peering over the rim and then retiring to one of the restaurants or snack bars along the rim or searching for souvenirs in a gift shop.

College and medical school studies interfered with a visit to Grand Canyon during the period 1966 to 1974—years of great tumult in the United States. Lyndon Johnson's attempt to form a Great Society foundered, America's involvement in Vietnam escalated, Martin Luther King and Bobby Kennedy were murdered, and Richard Nixon failed to unite us and eventually abandoned the presidency in shame. After completing my undergraduate studies in Boulder in 1970, I entered medical school at the University of Kansas School of Medicine in Kansas City, Kansas, where I met Ruth, a physical therapy student at Kansas University, and convinced her to stay in Kansas, marry me, and support me through my final three years of medical school.

Completion of my medical school studies at the University of Kansas in May 1974 (with internship not scheduled to start until late June) afforded me the opportunity to return to Grand Canyon. Ruth, my wife of three years, would join in the adventure. Three other couples signed on for the hike—Jay Curtis, an education major at KU in Lawrence, and his wife Becky, a nursing student at KU Medical Center; Roger and Mary Kathol, fellow medical students at KU; and Paul Edstrom (my roommate during my junior and senior years at CU) and his wife Kathy, both Denver residents. The common denominator for the group was their friendship with Ruth and me.

Although she was not a novice to hiking, this was Ruth's first trip to Grand Canyon. Ruth and I had backpacked several times in the Rocky Mountains of Colorado, including a summit of Mount Eolus, a fourteener in the Needles Mountains between Durango and Silverton. Likewise, the other couples had hiking experience but had never hiked in Grand Canyon. I had become an evangelist for the Grand Canyon and Ruth, the Edstroms, the Kathols, and the Curtises were my first converts.

John Muir said, "Nature has a few big places beyond man's power to spoil, the ocean, the two icy ends of the globe, and the Grand Canyon." Little did he know about man's ability to trash the earth. Beginning in 1971, the National Park Service required reservations and permits for camping below the rim in an attempt to limit damage to the environment by overuse by human visitors.

I contacted the backcountry office at the Grand Canyon months in advance of our hike in order to secure campground reservations. The Park Service also banned wood fires, requiring campers to carry small camp stoves and fuel for cooking. This trip I carried a new Camptrails brand external-frame pack. This pack featured padded shoulder straps and a hip belt to distribute some of the weight of the pack to my waist—incredible innovations in pack comfort—and similar to what I considered the holy grail of backpacks, the external-frame pack manufactured by Kelty. An open-cell foam camping pad replaced my air mattress. Although bulkier than an air mattress, the new camping pad was puncture proof.

I planned an ambitious expedition for late May 1974—a seven-day double traverse of the Canyon starting at the South Rim. Our route took us down the South Kaibab Trail (average grade of 21 percent) to Bright Angel Campground on the Colorado River and up the North Kaibab Trail (average grade of 21 percent) to the North Rim (with an intermediate stop at Cottonwood Campground). After a night on the North Rim we would retrace our steps to the river (camping at Roaring Springs and Bright Angel Campgrounds on the southbound trip), and return to the South Rim via the longer, but not as steep (average grade of 14 percent), Bright Angel Trail (camping at Indian Garden the last night in the Canyon). These trails were the maintained main corridor trails and were the only trails between Navajo Bridge to the east and Hoover Dam to the west leading to bridges across the Colorado River.

The three Kansas City couples met Paul and Kathy at Mather Campground on the South Rim on the evening prior to starting the hike. Early the next morning we distributed the food (predominately dehydrated products), pots and pans, two Svea camp stoves, and extra fuel canisters, stuffed everything we needed for a seven-day camping trip into our packs, and drove to the South Kaibab trailhead. Fearing neither rain nor insects and not wanting to carry any more weight than necessary, we left our tents in the trunks of our cars.

South Kaibab Trail starts on the western side of Yaki Point, four miles east of Grand Canyon Village. The rim is 7,260 feet in elevation at this point, and our destination that day was Bright Angel Campground—4,800 feet below us and 6.4 miles down the trail. The South Kaibab Trail was constructed in the 1920s by the National Park Service to compete with Cameron's Bright Angel Trail and provided alternative access to the inner canyon and the Colorado River from the South Rim. It was the only trail in the Canyon built by the National Park Service, costing $73,000 to build, a bargain even in today's dollars.

The trail ended at the Kaibab Suspension Bridge (river mile marker 87.4).

Unlike most trails in the Grand Canyon, which stay within the confines of a side canyon, the South Kaibab Trail followed open ridgelines that provided panoramic views of the main gorge and, except for a two-mile section into the inner gorge, was built where no previous trail existed. The views up and down the Canyon were spectacular from the South Kaibab Trail—an endless succession of pyramids, buttes, and mesas on both sides of the Colorado River. Although most of these features received titles by previous explorers, naturalists, and geologists, I had made no effort to learn a single name.

Our thighs burned from the steep descent to our first camp at Bright Angel Campground on the north side of the Colorado River. Despite our pain, we looked good, as we sported identical bright yellow T-shirts emblazoned with BIRUJAMA BEROPAKA, the first two letters of each of our first names, an idea developed by the three Kansas City couples over beer and burgers several weeks before the trip. Other Canyon hikers constantly queried us as to what organization we belonged. Unable to think of a brilliant but believable answer and reluctant to expose the boring truth, we simply shrugged our shoulders and said, "None."

Bright Angel Campground had changed little since my visit in 1961, except that more people were camping there and the sound of crackling campfires was replaced by the hissing of white gas-fueled camp stoves. In the intervening thirteen years backpacking had become a popular recreational endeavor and Grand Canyon had become a popular place to hike. Sporting goods stores now featured backpacking equipment in addition to basketballs, footballs, and baseball gloves and bats. Specialty backpacking and mountaineering stores were sprouting up around the country to feed the appetites of outdoor enthusiasts.

In 1961, most of the trail traffic I viewed was on mule back; I observed few hikers on the North Kaibab Trail and not many more on the Bright Angel Trail south of the river. After completion of my first traverse in 1961, I received loud praise about my remarkable achievement. By 1974, hundreds of individuals were hiking rim-to-rim—still an achievement, but not a rarity—and seldom would you find a vacant campsite along the main corridor trails during the popular spring and fall hiking seasons.

It was difficult to take the first few steps the morning of day two. The muscles of my calves and thighs were tender to the lightest touch. I had bruises on my shoulders and hips from the pressure of shoulder straps and hip belt. Medical school provided exercise for the mind but did not prepare my body for the hike. My seven hiking partners expressed no sympathy for my condition, as they suffered the same aches and pains. With a great deal of moaning and groaning we loaded our packs and slowly started the relatively flat 7.3 miles of North Kaibab Trail between Bright Angel Campground and Cottonwood Campground at 4,080 feet in elevation. The heat, not the climb, would be our enemy this day. After walking for several hours along Bright Angel Creek, we detoured to Ribbon Falls, a short trek to the west off the main trail, where we ate lunch, soaked our hot feet in the cool water, and rested in the cool mist generated by the falls. Becky and Jay nursed a growing crop of blisters on their feet, a consequence of stiff leather boots.

Ribbon Falls is a two-tiered fall approximately one hundred and twenty feet high. It emerged from a slot, dropped over a lip, and cascaded down a huge moss-covered travertine cone to the canyon floor. We climbed up to a wide ledge behind the falls and took midday naps in the shade of the overhang. With afternoon temperatures exceeding the century mark none of us were interested in starting the final mile to Cottonwood Campground until late afternoon.

During late spring, summer, and early fall months, savvy hikers avoid hiking in the inner canyon or climbing out of the Canyon between 11:00 AM and 4:00 PM, preferring to hike in the cooler early morning hours and in the late afternoon and evening. Hikers often arose well before sunrise to start climbing out of the Canyon or waited until late afternoon to start a descent into the Canyon. A hiker ignoring the advice to rest in the shade during the heat of the day probably carried insufficient water for the trek—a setup for heat exhaustion and heat stroke—the predominant cause of death due to the environment in the Grand Canyon.

Once Bright Angel Canyon was bathed in shadows we left the cool environs of Ribbon Falls and plodded on to Cottonwood Campground. Here we quickly stripped to our underwear and washed off the canyon dust in the chilly waters of Bright Angel Creek. After a less-than-gourmet meal of macaroni and cheese, Paul Edstrom read to us from

Colin Fletcher's book, *The Man Who Walked Through Time*. Published in 1968, Fletcher's book described his two-month walk through the Canyon in 1963, which occurred two years after my first hike in Grand Canyon. Fletcher is acknowledged as the first man to walk the entire length of Grand Canyon National Park below the rim from one end to the other in one continuous trip (in 1963 the park boundaries were Havasu Canyon on the west and Nankoweap Canyon on the east—one hundred four river miles). His book was not an adventure story or guidebook; rather, Fletcher wrote about his immersion into time and humankind's connection with nature. Paul's reading from Fletcher's book reinforced what we had discovered from our first two days in the Canyon.

Fletcher, who many consider the father of modern backpacking, also wrote *The Complete Walker,* an authoritative discourse on the techniques of hiking and backpacking. Known as the hiker's bible, *The Complete Walker* contained invaluable advice on what and how to pack for a backpacking trip. Fletcher's book was an indispensable resource for preparing for this and future hikes.

From Cottonwood we climbed 6.8 miles to the North Rim, nearly 4.200 vertical feet higher. Except for Roaring Springs I recognized little from my hike down North Kaibab Trail in 1961. In 1966 heavy rains flooded much of the trail in Roaring Springs Canyon, requiring construction of a new trail, including a bridge across a dry gorge in the Redwall.

Though tough going uphill, the higher we climbed the cooler it became. Ruth and I were the first in the group to the top. Paul and Roger finished next—running the final one hundred yards with loaded packs—reliving old times as competitors in track (Paul ran for Colorado University and Roger ran for Kansas University, where he garnered All American honors on the 4 x 1 mile relay team with Jim Ryun). Paul and Roger ran back down the trail and helped their wives with their packs. Hampered by blisters and poor conditioning, Becky and Jay preferred a slower pace climbing the steep trail through Roaring Springs Canyon and joined us on the rim much later. Once reunited, we walked another one and a half miles along the rim to reach the campground near Grand Canyon Lodge.

Arriving on the North Rim on Memorial Day weekend, we found the campground crowded and noisy. The Marty Robbins tune "El Paso" blared from someone's stereo speakers and the smoke of wood fires and the fragrance of Ponderosa pines wafted in the breeze. After procuring a campsite several members of our group walked to the nearby general store and purchased fresh fruit to supplement our diet of reconstituted dehydrated delicacies.

Cool temperatures greeted us on the forested Kaibab Plateau of the North Rim, and for the first time on the hike, we appreciated packing our sweatshirts and down sleeping bags. The Paiutes called the Kaibab Plateau *Kaiuw A-vwi,* or "Mountain Lying Down." Instead of mountain peaks the landscape was one of meadows and forest.

The next morning there was a nip to the air and frost on the ground. After a hearty breakfast of pancakes, the trek back to the South Rim commenced. We quickly descended 4.7 miles down North Kaibab trail to Roaring Springs Campground (5,200 feet in elevation), our first overnight stop on the trip south. In 1974 overnight camping was allowed at Roaring Springs, but it has since been designated for day use only. This relatively short hike put us in camp early—leaving plenty of time to relax, explore the springs, and play a lengthy game of charades. Roaring Springs is the major source of water for both the North and South Rims and a pumping station is located nearby to deliver water to the rims. A manager lived at Roaring Springs year 'round to supervise the operation. The springs takes its name from the roar it makes exiting the canyon wall—a noise that can be heard from Bright Angel Point on the rim, approximately 3,000 feet above the springs.

Our fifth day presented few challenges—a gentle downhill walk along Bright Angel Creek to Bright Angel Campground on the Colorado River. After five days on the trail I struggled with remembering what day of the week it was and discovered the pleasure of not knowing what bad things were happening in the world. A Canyon trek provided an escape from the tumult of modern life.

Before dawn of the sixth day we were on the trail, wanting to exit the inner canyon before it became unbearably hot. We crossed the river on the Bright Angel Bridge, also known as the Silver Bridge, a half mile downstream from the Kaibab Suspension Bridge. The Silver Bridge, constructed in the mid-1960s, supported the transcanyon water pipeline crossing the Colorado River on its long journey from Roaring Springs, down Bright Angel Canyon, and up to the South Rim. The pipeline supplied Grand Canyon Village on the South Rim with 500,000 gallons of water a day. For much of the way from Roaring Springs to the Colorado River, the pipe carrying water to the South Rim was buried under the North Kaibab Trail.

A short walk in the relative cool of the morning ended at Indian Garden. The Edstroms and the Kathols lobbied to finish the climb to the rim that day, while Becky, Jay, Ruth, and I preferred to stay at Indian Garden as originally planned. I was not ready to leave the Canyon. I wanted to view the sunset from Plateau Point, a mile-and-a-half walk north from Indian Garden. After a brief and not always cordial discussion, we decided to camp at Indian Garden and hike out early the next morning.

The sun arced across the Tonto Plateau, and the shadows cast by the cottonwoods at Indian Garden slowly circled from west to east. Seeking the relative comfort in the shade and tired from six days of hiking, we limited our physical activity during the heat of the day to following the shadows. As evening approached the four couples walked to Plateau Point, where we observed the antics of canyon swallows and witnessed a beautiful sunset.

The seventh day brought rest, but not until climbing out of the Canyon. After six days of hiking we felt strong and had adjusted to the altitude. The 4.6-mile hike from Indian Garden at 3,800 feet in elevation to Grand Canyon Village, 3,000 vertical feet higher, presented no difficulties. Becky and Jay, who always lagged behind during the first six days of the hike, uncharacteristically led the way.

In seven days we hiked over fifty miles with full packs, gaining and losing over 21,000 vertical feet. Like a highlight film capturing the finest moments of a championship basketball season, a transcanyon hike afforded us the opportunity to observe many of the classic features of the Grand Canyon. Walking from the high desert environment of the South Rim to the alpine meadows and forests of the North Rim, we descended and ascended through the multiple layers of rock telling the geologic history of the Canyon. We actually touched the canyon walls that most visitors to the Canyon only see from the rims. In addition to seeing the Colorado River, we heard its roar. Our group walked beside, bathed in, and drank the crystal clear waters of a stream racing down a narrow side canyon, witnessed sunrise and sunset from multiple vantage points, baked in the heat in the inner canyon at midday, inhaled trail dust from rim to river, slept on the hard earth of the Canyon floor, and viewed temples and buttes from above and below. Everyone departed the Canyon with blistered feet, sore, tired muscles, sunburns, red dust in their clothes, boots, and nostrils, and, hopefully, a deeper appreciation of their connection with nature.

Chapter 4
Rim-to-Rim-to-Rim, Again

May 1989

> *It is generally conceded that the Grand Canyon beggars description. I shall therefore endeavor to refrain from doing so. Right here at the outset I realize that this is going to be a considerable contract. Nearly everybody, on taking a first look at the Grand Canyon, comes right out and admits its wonders are absolutely indescribable—and then proceeds to write anywhere from two thousand to fifty thousand words, giving the full details. Speaking personally, I wish to say that I do not know anybody who has yet succeeded in getting away with the job.*

> **—Irvin S. Cobb, "Roughing It Deluxe," 1913**

Jack Gibbens, a friend from Merriam, Kansas, and I had just entered The Box, a narrow, 1,200-foot deep inner gorge in the Vishnu Complex of Bright Angel Canyon above Phantom Ranch, on a brilliant early-May morning in 1989. I turned to Jack and quietly urged him to quicken the pace to see if my friend and fellow physician from Salina, Ray Schmidt, would stay with us. Ray did not respond to the sudden change in pace. He had no intention of wearing himself out on the second day of a five-day trek in the Canyon. Perhaps in the best physical shape in our lives, Jack and I relished the brisk walk with full packs on the gentle incline beside Bright Angel Creek on the way to a proposed lunch stop at Ribbon Falls. I had just turned forty and was swimming, running, and biking regularly. Jack, ten years my senior, was also actively engaged in an exercise program. Ray was no slouch either. He kept fit through a regular program of jogging.

It had been fifteen years since my last hike in Grand Canyon. In that period I completed a three-year internal medicine residency at KU Medical Center in Kansas City, Kansas, and spent another twenty months in a clinical pharmacology fellowship at KU before moving to Salina, Kansas in 1979, and establishing a practice in internal medicine. In 1977, 1981, and 1987 Ruth and I welcomed children—Kate, John, and Elizabeth, respectively—into the world. During the long interval between Grand Canyon trips, my hikes were confined to the mountains of Colorado.

In October 1988, I visited both South and North Rims and rode my bike along the rim roads, but did not set foot below the rim. The yearning to strap on my boots, shoulder a pack, and head down the trail remained strong. I had an itch that only a hike in the Canyon could scratch. I never tired of viewing the Canyon from the rim, but its breadth and depth cannot be fully appreciated from the edge. All five senses are stimulated, often simultaneously, while walking in the Canyon. The visual beauty of the Canyon and the need to watch your step on a treacherous trail are obvious, but add the sound of footsteps on the path, the creak of backpack, and the rush of water over rocks, the pressure of feet on the ground and pack on the shoulders, the fragrance of streamside flora and the not so pleasant odor of puddles of mule urine, and the taste of salty sweat on your lips and the peculiar taste of water consumed from a plastic canteen that had once contained a variety of other flavored drinks, and you had sensory overload. Completing a hike is an accomplishment, but the walk itself is a joy. I understood what Thich Nhat Hanh meant by, "Happiness is not a point of arrival. Happiness is the way."

The day before Jack and I challenged Ray in The Box, the three of us started a double traverse of the Grand Canyon (rim-to-rim-to-rim, traveling from south to north to south)—a repeat of my walk of May 1974. I had hiked with Jack and Ray before, although this was the first trip the three of us hiked together. My friendship with Jack Gibbens dated to 1972, when Ruth and I met him at a small church we were attending in Overland Park, Kansas. Our friendship prospered even though Ruth and I eventually moved away from the Kansas City area. Jack had hiked with me in the Needles and Sangre de Cristo Mountains of Colorado in the early 1980s, but this was his first trip to Grand Canyon. Jack carried my old Camptrails backpack that I had sold to him. I finally had purchased the pack of my dreams, a Kelty Tioga external-frame backpack. The packsack was a beautiful azure blue with a huge main compartment for most of my gear and multiple side pockets to place my water bottles, a plastic drinking cup, and other miscellaneous items. To own a Kelty was to be among the hiking elite, or at least I thought it was.

I originally met Ray when he was in practice in Garden City, Kansas, where I spent a month during residency training in 1976. Ray moved his general surgery practice to Salina in 1978, and was among the first physicians to welcome me to town. Ray had hiked in Grand Canyon with his wife on one occasion many years before and had hiked with me in the Indian Peaks Wilderness Area of Colorado several years earlier.

Starting the trek at Yaki Point on the South Rim, Jack, Ray, and I hiked 4.4 miles down the South Kaibab Trail to its junction with the Tonto Trail on the Tonto Plateau or Platform. Instead of continuing down the South Kaibab Trail to the Colorado River we hiked west a distance of 4.5 miles on the relatively level but serpentine and sun-exposed Tonto Trail to Indian Garden. The cottonwoods along Pipe Creek provided a shady place to stop for lunch between the South Kaibab Trail and Indian Garden. Prior to completion of the River Trail in 1936, this section of the Tonto Trail was the sole link between the Bright Angel Trail and the South Kaibab Trail and was used to reach Phantom Ranch from Indian Garden.

The Tonto Trail neither started nor ended at the rim. The eastern end of the trail started along the Colorado River at Red Canyon near Hance Rapids (river mile 76.5) and the western end was located on the south bank of the river at Elves Chasm (river mile 116.6) in Garnet Canyon (U.S.G.S. maps: Cape Royal, Phantom Ranch, Grand Canyon, Shiva Temple, Piute Point, Havasupai Point, Explorers Monument). For most of its ninety-mile length the trail ran along the Tonto Platform, a bench in the Bright Angel Shale above the inner gorge. The Tonto Trail winds in and out of drainages and was the longest continuous stretch of trail in the Grand Canyon. It was created and used by the various Native Americans that once inhabited the Canyon. Traveling east to west the Tonto Trail crossed the New Hance Trail, South Kaibab Trail, Bright Angel Trail, Hermit Trail, Boucher Trail, and South Bass Trail. Each of these trails offered access to the South Rim.

Our first night's camp at Indian Garden teemed with kids on school-sponsored field trips. I carried fresh onions and garlic and cans of tomatoes and garbanzo beans and prepared garbanzo bean spaghetti for dinner. After our evening meal we walked one and a half miles to Plateau Point and joined a number of other hikers perched on the lip of the inner canyon to watch the sunset.

Ray packed a lightweight four-person tent, but we chose to leave it in his pack, preferring to sleep without shelter. Ray slept on the flat surface of a picnic table at our campsite rather than on the ground. I never asked why Ray chose the picnic table as a place to sleep, but worried he would roll over in the night, joining us on the ground and injuring himself in the fall.

By dawn of day two, our trio was on the trail, hiking down Bright Angel Trail to the River Trail along the Colorado River. A short walk on the south side of the river brought us to the Silver Bridge, our link to the north side of the river and the North Kaibab Trail. Our goal that day was Cottonwood Campground (4,080 feet in elevation), where we would camp for two nights.

I enjoyed hiking in the early morning hours—a time of cooler air temperature, a quiet time before most other hikers had started down the trail, a time of rapid changes in the light and canyon colors as the sun peeked over the rim, a time when my strength and energy were at their peak. Although I loved my family and, for the most part, enjoyed my career as a physician, it was great to temporarily remove myself from that world and immerse myself in a different world.

Jack, Ray, and I hiked together until just above Phantom Ranch where Jack and I literally left Ray in the dust. The two jackrabbits reached Ribbon Falls one hour ahead of Ray, who was satisfied that he had saved his energy for another day.

After lunch and a lengthy rest period at the base of Ribbon Falls we moseyed on to Cottonwood Campground. In contrast to a crowded, noisy Indian Garden Campground, Cottonwood was deserted. Darkness enveloped camp as we sat on a large boulder beside Bright Angel Creek, enjoying the coolness along the water's edge and sipping after dinner cocktails prepared from Tang and distilled spirits supplied by Ray. It was one of those moments I will never forget—sitting by the rushing stream at nightfall in the depths of the Canyon, listening to the night noises, and enjoying the company of good friends after a great day of hiking in a place I love.

Day three meant a long walk—from Cottonwood to the North Rim and back. Carrying only trail snacks and water bottles in fanny packs instead of heavy backpacks, we made good time climbing out of the Canyon. On the ascent we passed two young men repairing washed out sections of the trail. They reassured us that the trail was open to the rim.

This early in the season we met no other pedestrians on the trail. Upon reaching the rim we walked to Grand Canyon Lodge located nearly two miles south of the trailhead. The lodge was not officially open; however, workers were preparing the facilities for the tourist season (mid-May to early October). Fortunately, the workmen had activated the water system, enabling us to fill our empty canteens. Unavailability of potable water at the lodge would have forced us to melt snow drifted along the road between the trailhead and Grand Canyon Lodge to quench our thirst.

From Grand Canyon Lodge we walked the short distance to Bright Angel Point and surveyed our route through Bright Angel Canyon below us. The Colorado River was hidden in the inner gorge, but we could readily identify the severe narrowing of Bright Angel Canyon known as The Box. On the south horizon lie the South Rim and the Coconino Plateau. Although imperceptible to the human eye, at Bright Angel Point we stood 1,200 feet higher in elevation than the South Rim. It was nearly twice as far from the North Rim to the Colorado River as from the river to the South Rim. The southward slope of the Colorado Plateau through which the Colorado River cut caused more runoff to enter the canyon from the north side, resulting in more erosion north of the river.

After taking the obligatory pictures from Bright Angel Point, Jack, Ray, and I hustled back down the trail to our camp at Cottonwood, completing nearly seventeen miles of travel between dawn and dusk. During our absence a varmint had chewed through the fabric of my new Kelty pack to snack on the dried apricots and Beer Nuts stored inside, despite the fact that my pack was properly suspended from a metal pole erected at the campground. Obviously this intruder could jump. I did not fret over the loss of the food as much as I did the damage to my precious pack.

Jack, Ray and Bill at Bright Angel Point

We hiked back to Bright Angel Campground the next day—with the usual intermediate stop at Ribbon Falls during the afternoon heat. We spent a restless night at Bright Angel Campground because high temperatures and blowing dirt made for poor sleeping conditions.

Before daybreak on day five we left Bright Angel Campground to start our hike out of the Canyon. I decided to cross the river on the Kaibab Suspension Bridge and hike out alone on the steeper but shorter South Kaibab Trail to our car at the trailhead at Yaki Point. In addition to being steeper than the Bright Angel Trail, the South Kaibab Trail had no shade or sources of water. These factors contributed to its unpopularity as an exit route from the inner canyon in late spring, summer, and early fall. The climb out did not seem so daunting if I approached it as a walk up the stairs from ground level to the top of the Empire State Building—three and a third times. The Empire State Building is nearly 1,454 feet tall (one hundred two stories) and there are 1,860 steps (7.5 inches per step) to the top. I only had 7,680 steps to go. I felt sufficiently robust this morning and was confident that this route would not be too taxing in the cool hours of the early morning, as long as I carried plenty of water.

Jack and Ray had no problem with my plan, but they had a different plan. Not as confident about their strength and endurance, they elected to cross the river on the Silver Bridge and hike 9.3 miles to the rim on the River and Bright Angel Trails. These trails were not as steep as the South Kaibab Trail, and drinking water sources existed at Indian Garden and at two rest houses between Indian Garden and the rim.

A fast pace and a shorter route put me on the rim long before Jack and Ray. I recovered our vehicle at the trailhead, showered at Mather campground, ate breakfast, purchased groceries for our drive back to Kansas, drove to Grand Canyon Village, and still had to wait for Ray and Jack to emerge from the Canyon.

Sitting on the rock wall along the rim near Bright Angel Lodge, I scanned the enormous chasm. Bright Angel Point on the North Rim, where I had been three days earlier, lay a short ten miles across the canyon. I could easily see Indian Garden, the Tonto Plateau, and the trail to Plateau Point 3,000 feet below. The Colorado River, tucked in the inner gorge, was hidden from view. I never tired of this view, and I vowed not to let so many years elapse before returning. I realized that despite the energy expended hiking in the Canyon, the trek restored my energy to be a husband, father, and physician—and to pursue a growing interest in cancer medicine.

Chapter 5
Thunder River

September 1991

Experience is the name so many people give to their mistakes.

—Oscar Wilde

It is said that an adventure is a tragedy that doesn't happen. My fifth hike in Grand Canyon proved to be quite an adventure. It was my first hike through a designated wilderness area in Grand Canyon—a region where the land was left in a state minimally modified by humans—or as stated by National Park Service, "an area where the earth and its community of life are untrammeled by man, where man himself is a visitor who does not remain."

My wife Ruth and our friends from Salina, Glenda and Ray Schmidt, joined me for this adventure. Glenda had hiked in the Grand Canyon with Ray many years earlier, while Ray last hiked in the Canyon with Jack Gibbens and me in 1989. Ruth returned to Grand Canyon after a seventeen-year hiatus. I do not believe she made the hike out of a burning desire to see the Grand Canyon again. Rather, she made the trip out of a desire to accompany her husband on something he wanted to do. My interest in the Thunder River area was piqued after reading a brief description of a Thunder River trek sponsored by the Sierra Club.

Ready to venture off the main corridor trails, I was confident that I could lead such a trip. Like the sirens' call, Thunder River beckoned me.

My proposed route started at Monument Point on the North Rim, descended the Bill Hall Trail for two and a half miles to its junction with Thunder River Trail coming in from Indian Hollow to the north, continued south across the Esplanade on the Thunder River Trail, descended the Redwall into Surprise Valley, and headed east to Thunder Springs. From Thunder Springs a trail descended along Thunder River to Tapeats Creek before turning south along Tapeats Creek to the Colorado River. Upon reaching the river our course headed west along the river to Deer Creek before turning north up Deer Creek Trail to Deer Creek Valley and climbing east into Surprise Valley. The loop completed, we would retrace our steps up the Redwall across the Esplanade and out of the Canyon on the Bill Hall Trail (U.S.G.S. maps: Tapeats Amphitheater, Fishtail Mesa, Powell Plateau). None of these trails were maintained by National Park personnel or hired trail workers, as were the main corridor trails, but I did not expect problems finding our way.

We chose fall for the hike because Tapeats Creek crossings were difficult, if not impossible, during spring runoff, summers were brutally hot, and snow limited access to the trailhead during winter. The timing of the trip also provided me with a brief respite from studying for medical oncology boards scheduled for November.

On September 12, 1991, Ruth and I drove to Vail, Colorado, where we rendezvoused with Ray and Glenda. Another two days of driving brought us to the North Rim of Grand Canyon. After spending the night in one of Grand Canyon Lodge's rustic cabins, we drove north of Grand Canyon Lodge towards Jacob Lake. At Demotte Park, approximately five miles north of the park boundary, we headed northwest on Forest Road 422 until it intersected with Forest Road 425, then drove south on FR 425, and then FR 292 to the parking lot near Monument Point (7,206 feet in elevation).

My guidebook claimed the Bill Hall trailhead could be found by walking a half-mile west along the rim. The half-mile walk was easy, but finding the trailhead proved to be a difficult task. Ray and I scoured the area for over an hour looking for the entrance into the canyon.

We found only cattle paths coursing through the brush and piñon pines on the rim. Had I overestimated my trail-finding abilities? While we searched, the women removed their packs and sat in the shade, questioning the wisdom of the expedition. I foolishly refused to remove my pack during the rummage along the rim, certain that the trailhead would be found momentarily. Reminded of Yogi Berra's advice, "You've got to be very careful if you don't know where you're going, because you may not get there," I confessed to being at least temporarily disoriented. Ruth begged to differ, claiming her husband was flat-out lost. To which Yogi would have responded, "We're lost, but we're making good time." We were lost and had yet to step below the canyon rim, an inauspicious start to our trip.

Backtracking to Monument Point, we started our search anew. Finally I sighted a small pile of rocks near the canyon's edge. Upon further investigation I discovered the start of the descent down Bill Hall Trail. What a magnificent view from the trailhead, Bridgers Knoll to the south, the broad expanse of the Esplanade below us to the right, and Great Thumb Mesa on the South Rim on the horizon. What a pain in the butt that it had taken us so long to find it.

The first steps foreshadowed the difficulty to come. We had to remove our packs and carefully climb down a steep rock face to actually set foot on the trail. Once on firm footing on the trail, packs were lowered by the trailing hiker into the outreached hands of those below.

The walk through the two upper layers of the Canyon (Kaibab Limestone and Toroweap Formation) was steep and at times treacherous because of loose rock on the trail—each of us slipped on our back sides a couple of times. We continued the descent through the Coconino Sandstone and Hermit Shale. Our legs became rubbery from several hours of downhill walking with heavy packs—and I had unwisely carried my pack an extra hour on the rim. Ray cached a gallon jug of water, clearly labeled with his name and the date, in low shrubs near the junction of the Hermit Shale and the Esplanade. He dutifully recorded its location in a pocket notebook. We planned to retrieve and use the water on the hike out, as there were no water sources above either Thunder Springs or Deer Creek, both eight miles from the trailhead.

The path leveled upon reaching the Esplanade and merged with the Thunder River Trail coming in from Indian Hollow to the north.

The Esplanade, an expansive plateau in the uppermost member of the Supai Group in the western Grand Canyon, was a land of red earth, mushroom rocks, sparse vegetation, and level walking—wide-open country rather than a confining side canyon, like Bright Angel Canyon or the Inner Gorge. A short distance beyond the merger of the Bill Hall Trail with the Thunder River Trail, we made our first wilderness camp, pitching identical blue lightweight two-person tents on the red earth and starting twin Svea stoves to cook dinner. Our voices and the hissing stoves were the only noises to pierce an otherwise silent evening.

We saw no other hikers from the time we left the parking lot near Monument Point until the morning of the second day, when a couple climbing to the rim stopped to wish us well as we were leaving camp. They gave us an extra jug of water, a copy of George Steck's book *Grand Canyon Loop Trails I*, and a walking stick. Ruth and Glenda already had walking sticks and Ray did not want one, so I gladly accepted it. I found the walking staff an indispensable tool when going downhill with a heavy pack. It helped with balance and lessened the stress on my legs, as I carried a recently purchased North Face internal-frame pack loaded with nearly sixty pounds of gear. In addition to the usual camping essentials I packed a video camera, canned tomatoes, and garbanzo beans for a trail dinner, a liter of red wine, a gallon jug of water to cache above the Redwall for the trip out, and another five quarts of water for the trip to Thunder Springs.

After departing our first night's camp, we hiked several miles south-southwest across the Esplanade—following a trail defined by rock cairns placed at irregular intervals on the red rock surface. The trail crossed expansive slickrock sections as it wound around several small drainages. There was no well-worn path to follow, and at times I found it challenging to differentiate between randomly scattered rocks and true trail markers. Luckily, I knew we needed to head in a southerly direction.

At the south end of the Esplanade near the start of the Redwall Limestone, I cached my gallon jug of water in a rock crevice. The Redwall is naturally blue gray in color but is superficially stained by the truly red-colored rock layers above, the Hermit Shale and Supai Formation.

We descended a series of switchbacks through the bottom layers of the Supai Formation and through the Redwall Limestone to Surprise Valley in the Muav Limestone. Surprise Valley may have received its name from its unusual bowl shape and nearly hidden outlet through Bonito Creek at its south end. According to geologists, Surprise Valley was the result of a rotational landslide or slump. Known for its heat and aridity, Surprise Valley was not a place to be stranded on a hot day with no water.

In the upper reaches of Surprise Valley the trail divided—the western spur going to Deer Creek, and the eastern spur to Thunder Springs. This was the start of the loop hike, although when traced on a map, our route looked more rectangular than circular. We headed east, walking approximately a mile and a half east across the level floor of Surprise Valley before climbing a short rise and descending to Thunder Springs. The roar of Thunder Springs could be heard before actually sighting it.

Thunder Springs was a tropical paradise in the desert southwest. The jet engine-like roar of water exiting from tunnels in the Redwall was deafening—the springs were appropriately named. Hanging gardens surrounded the springs. The cool mist generated by the springs provided relief from the heat. The water from Thunder Springs formed Thunder River—allegedly the "world's shortest river" (a half-mile long) emptying into a creek (Tapeats Creek). Cottonwoods shaded the river and along its banks grew crimson monkey flowers and maidenhair ferns.

From Thunder Springs the trail descended 1,000 feet in one mile along the south bank of Thunder River to our second night's camp (Upper Tapeats Campground) located just below the junction of Thunder River with Tapeats Creek. That night we feasted on garbanzo bean pasta, hummus, pita bread, and a bottle of cabernet sauvignon, sharing leftovers with two young men camped near by. They were impressed with the quality of our cuisine, and even more impressed that we had bothered to carry heavy cans and a bottle of wine for a camp dinner in a remote area of the Grand Canyon.

Bill and Ruth on the Thunder River Trail in The Redwall

On the morning of the third day of our expedition Ray and I hiked a couple of miles up Tapeats Creek—no goal in mind other than casual exploration. Glenda and Ruth chose to stay in camp and rest. Tapeats Creek is the largest creek originating in the Grand Canyon. There was no clearly identifiable trail going upstream, so we walked along one side of the creek until an obstacle forced us to cross to the opposite bank. At first, Ray and I tried to keep our shoes and socks dry by removing them and fording the shallow creek in bare feet. After several crossings we tired of the process, preferring to leave our boots on for creek crossings. Finally, we abandoned dry land and sloshed upstream in the shallow water. Upon reaching the union of two smaller tributaries to form the main channel, Ray and I declared our exploration at an end and headed back to camp.

After returning to camp and enjoying a light lunch and short naps, we hiked south for approximately two and a half miles along Tapeats Creek to its confluence with the Colorado River (river mile marker 133.6). The trail crossed Tapeats Creek several times between Upper Tapeats Campground and the river. Neither the depth nor swiftness of the water deterred Ray and me from fording the stream without hesitation. However, at each crossing Ruth and Glenda changed into water shoes and cautiously waded across the knee-deep water, allowing Ray and me to portage their packs across. The women did not want to risk falling in the stream with loaded packs. After each crossing the women changed back to dry socks and boots and proceeded with the journey.

Approximately a mile from the river the trail abruptly ended at a rock wall. Somehow we had managed to take a dead end spur. Ray peered over the cliff on the right-hand side of the trail and sighted a path six to eight feet below us. Despite backtracking a short distance, a connection with the trail below us could not be found, and we were forced to improvise. Using small hand and foot holds in the cliff face we climbed down to the path and continued along the creek bank towards the river. Just before Tapeats Creek plunged into a lower gorge we made a final crossing of the fast moving stream and followed the trail traversing high above the gorge before it precipitously plunged down a steep talus slope to Lower Tapeats Campground on the Colorado River. That night we pitched our tents on a sandy beach near a group of river rafters—the roar of the river drowning out all but the closest of voices.

Shortly after dawn of day four we headed west along the Colorado River, threading between boulders or hopping from boulder to boulder—a tedious job. It did not take much of this to tire us out. A trail existed somewhere, but I failed to find it. Once again my companions questioned my talents as a guide. I had hoped to cover the estimated three to four land miles (2.6 river miles) between Tapeats Creek and Deer Creek Canyon, the next major drainage to the west, in the relative cool of the morning and climb out of the inner gorge before it became brutally hot. At the slow pace we were progressing and the fast rate we were expending energy, my plan to reach Deer Creek by noon appeared to be only wishful thinking.

Less than a mile downriver the leader of a raft trip floated by and inquired if we would like to ride with him to Deer Creek Falls, where the trail leading up Deer Creek Canyon originated. Ruth and Glenda had met Roger at Upper Tapeats Campground the previous day (while Ray and I walked upstream), when he escorted a group of rafters up the Tapeats Creek drainage to view Thunder Springs. This morning he piloted an empty raft down the river. His charges had elected to walk upstream along Tapeats Creek to Thunder River, hike along Thunder River, climb to Surprise Valley, cross Surprise Valley and descend the Deer Creek drainage to the river before boarding the raft. Having never rafted on the Colorado River, we eagerly accepted his invitation. Bounding over boulders had ceased to be fun and a raft ride offered respite from walking, as well as a faster means of getting to Deer Creek.

We climbed aboard, dumped our packs on the raft floor, and donned life jackets—a requirement despite the fact that the river would be smooth the entire trip. Roger briefly halted the trip downriver to view Christmas Tree Cave, a huge alcove carved into the inner canyon wall by the river. After reboarding the rafts we floated through the eerily quiet Granite Narrows section of the inner gorge—the narrowest passageway the river takes in Grand Canyon. On average the river ran forty feet deep but ran a hundred to one hundred twenty feet deep as it cut through the Granite Narrows.

Disembarking upon reaching the beach at Deer Creek Falls, we thanked Roger and commenced the long walk back to Monument Point on the North Rim. Hundred-foot tall Deer Creek Falls splashed to the ground a short distance back from the Colorado River, forming a shallow creek that bisected the small beach at the foot of the falls and separated us from the trail out of the inner gorge.

Crossing Deer Creek near its union with the Colorado River, I looked back over my shoulder to see if Glenda needed a hand crossing the wet stones. For this shallow stream crossing she had decided not to remove her boots and pack. At just that moment, she slipped and fell—immediately crying out, "I've broken my ankle." Ray voiced disbelief that such a slip resulted in a fracture. "I know when my ankle is broken," Glenda curtly replied.

Broken or not, Glenda could not bear weight on her left ankle. Her hiking trip suddenly ended. She sat beside the stream, soaking her painful ankle in the cold water. I sat down next to her and wondered, *What in the hell are we going to do now?* Fortunately, Roger's rafting party provided a solution. Roger splinted Glenda's ankle and took Ray and Glenda aboard a raft and floated downriver, hoping to summon emergency medical care via a walkie-talkie to the outside world. When they would make such contact was unknown. Ruth and I would have to leave the Canyon on foot and try to communicate with Ray and Glenda after we climbed to the rim, collected the car, and located a phone.

Shaken by Glenda's mishap but having no alternative, Ruth and I climbed out of the inner gorge and headed north on Deer Creek Trail. The first part of the trail was dangerously narrow—my left shoulder rubbed against a rock wall and my right foot seemed dangerously close to the edge of a slot canyon carved into the Tapeats sandstone by Deer Creek. We avoided leaning over the edge to view the creek rushing through Deer Creek Narrows for fear of falling. The rushing water of Deer Creek sounded a long distance down. Ruth and I cautiously tight-roped along the narrow ledge for a short distance before the trail widened.

After hiking one and a half miles to the north along the west bank of Deer Creek, we forded the stream and climbed a short spur trail to Deer Springs, a tributary of Deer Creek. By 1:00 PM, we had progressed less than two miles from the river, and I felt very weak and tired.

Ruth promptly diagnosed early heat exhaustion and wisely advised a long break in the shade of the abundant foliage near the springs. We bivouacked for several hours, drinking our fill of pure, cold spring water and eating an early supper consisting of a dreadful oriental dish prepared by adding hot water to a foil pouch of noodles, dehydrated chicken and spices. Deer Springs was our last source of water, except for cached supplies, until we were out of the Canyon—a distance of approximately 9.5 miles.

The shadows lengthened, and I regained my strength and desire to continue. Ruth and I filled all of our water containers to the brim at the springs, shouldered our packs, and climbed a steep unnamed drainage into Surprise Valley, a distance estimated at two miles. Surprise Valley proved a much cooler place at dusk than in the late morning two days earlier. On our final night in the Canyon, we pitched our tent in central Surprise Valley near the junction of the trail heading east to Thunder River. The ends of the loop were joined. We could see or hear no other human visitors to Surprise Valley. The dark walls of the canyon framed a starry sky. Only the rustle of breeze through low scrub was heard. I fell asleep wondering what fate had befallen Ray and Glenda.

On the morning of day five, I slowly packed our gear while Ruth videotaped my labors and the geologic features of Surprise Valley. Once loaded, we completed the walk across Surprise Valley and ascended the steep switchbacks through the Redwall. After recovering our water cache just beyond the top of the Redwall, Ruth and I retraced the path on the Esplanade, exchanging few words on the long, level leg of the journey. Only the sounds of footsteps and breathing disturbed the silence, providing lots of time to think and daydream. Our water cache near the junction of the Hermit Shale and the Esplanade could not be found—apparently confiscated by another hiking party. Hopefully they needed it more than Ruth and I did, as we had sufficient water for the remainder of our hike.

Ruth and I climbed through the Hermit Shale, the steep talus slope of Coconino Sandstone, the Toroweap Formation, and finally the Kaibab Limestone to the top—counting nearly sixty switchbacks from Esplanade to rim. During the twenty-four hours since leaving Deer Springs we saw only one person—a solo male hiker on the upper reaches of the Bill Hall Trail. Ruth questioned the wisdom of hiking solo in this inhospitable environment. With Glenda's mishap fresh in her mind, she asked, "What if he broke his ankle?"

"He's dead meat," I countered.

This had truly been an adventure, an exceedingly agreeable experience, despite Glenda's injury. Fortunately, her fall occurred close to river runners who assisted with her evacuation.

Except for a solar composting toilet at Upper Tapeats campground, no manmade structures marred the landscape on our journey. For a brief time we escaped to a place of unspoiled natural beauty and silence, a place where one could be alone but not lonely. The quiet of Surprise Valley and the Esplanade was particularly noteworthy—no babble of streams, no roar of river, and few human voices to disturb the silence—only the occasional whisper of the wind. I agreed with Sigurd Olson, who wrote in *Reflections from the North Country* that two of the greatest values of wilderness travel are solitude and silence. In an essay commemorating the fortieth anniversary of Thomas Merton's death, Frederick Smock, chair of the English Department at Bellarmine University in Louisville, Kentucky, wrote that when we are silent, we are more attuned to the natural world around us.

I discovered something new about hiking in the Canyon. It was not just a rugged place to challenge a physically fit human. This place challenged me to appreciate my vulnerable position as a minute organism in a huge, often hostile world. It also challenged me to converse with myself during long periods of silence on the trail—and to listen to the quiet. The Quakers had it right. A time of silence allows the divine to speak in the heart and mind.

Several hours after climbing out of the Canyon, I made telephone contact with Ray Schmidt. He and Glenda spent nearly twenty-four hours with the rafters before Roger made radio contact with a sightseeing plane over the Canyon. The National Park Service sent a helicopter to evacuate Ray and Glenda. X-rays at Grand Canyon Village confirmed a fracture of Glenda's left ankle. Glenda was taken to Flagstaff for surgery, and after recovery she was released to fly home. Ray and Glenda's adventure ended differently than Ruth's and mine, but tragedy had been averted.

Chapter 6
A Father and Son Walk

March 1993

For Christmas 1961, a few months following my first hike in Grand Canyon, my parents gave me a copy of *Brighty of the Grand Canyon* by Marguerite Henry. It chronicled the adventures of a burro, Brighty, as he roamed from rim to rim in Grand Canyon. Although perhaps intended for an elementary school reader, it rekindled memories of my first hike in the Canyon. Ruth and I had read this book to our children when they were young. I remember one summer in the late 1980s at our cabin in Colorado when every afternoon before naps John and Kate would excitedly clamber onto our bed to hear about Brighty—and the Grand Canyon.

I enjoyed telling my kids about the Grand Canyon and wanted to share with them the experience of hiking in it, hoping they would find it a special place too. My love of camping and hiking was not something passed down to me from my dad. His idea of roughing it was staying in a motel that had seen better days. However, I was conscious of the hardships he faced growing up on a small family farm near Tecumseh, Kansas, during the Great Depression—the heat, dust and insects of summer, the cold of winter, and chores before and after school—and I suspect growing up in that environment was roughing it for him.

Mentors like Jack McDavid introduced me to the wonders of the outdoors. I took it upon myself to introduce my children to the joys of hiking and camping in the wild. Although not averse to exercise, my oldest daughter Kate declined my offer to take her hiking in the Grand Canyon. She and John had hiked with me in the Lost Park Wilderness Area near our cabin in South Park, Colorado. John enjoyed the outing but Kate found it thoroughly unpleasant.

John's first trip to the Canyon occurred in March 1993, several months before he turned twelve. My son was much more athletic than I was at that age and he was not intimidated by the prospect of a long walk in the Grand Canyon. A simple excursion from the South Rim to the Colorado River and back—with a side trip to Ribbon Falls—seemed like a great introductory hike. John and I flew from Wichita to Phoenix, rented a car, and drove to the South Rim of the Grand Canyon, spending the night at Bright Angel Lodge before our hike.

John on the South Rim

We entered the Canyon on the South Kaibab Trail near Yaki Point—my usual point of entry from the South Rim when going to Bright Angel Campground. John carried a small backpack containing the bare essentials (sleeping bag, sleeping pad, a jacket, and a change of socks), leaving me to carry the tent, food, stove, fuel, cook pots, and my personal camping gear. John and I quickly dropped below the rim in a tight set of switchbacks in the Kaibab Formation known as The Chimney and slowly descended to Cedar Ridge before taking a break. Devoid of any cedars, how did it get its name? Perhaps it should be called Piñon Point or Juniper Point after the trees that did grow there. The South Kaibab Trail skirted O'Neill Butte and then followed a ridge to Skeleton Point at the top of the Redwall, where we viewed the river nearly 3,000 feet below. After a series of switchbacks in the Redwall and a steep descent through the Muav Limestone, John and I reached the Tonto Plateau and blessed level ground—bringing relief to my burning thighs—although only briefly, as the trail once more assumed a steeper pitch to the river.

By early afternoon John and I crossed the Colorado River on the Kaibab Suspension Bridge on the way to Bright Angel Campground, established in the 1930s by the Civilian Conservation Corps. Bright Angel Campground lay along the west bank of Bright Angel Creek and consisted of thirty-three separate campsites. An access trail divided a string of campsites along the creek from another string of campsites abutting the sheer wall of schist to the west. Campsites were separated from each other by a row of willows.

Bright Angel Campground was one of many conservation and construction projects completed by the Civilian Conservation Corps, created in 1933 by FDR to provide jobs for indigent, unemployed young men. Nationwide the CCC planted three billion trees, constructed 28,000 miles of trail, and erected 63,000 buildings during its lifespan, which ended in 1942. The CCC made many infrastructural improvements in Grand Canyon. In addition to Bright Angel Campground they built the rock wall along the rim between the El Tovar Hotel and Bright Angel Lodge on the South Rim, landscaped Grand Canyon Village, improved Bright Angel Trail, constructed the River, Clear Creek, Ribbon Falls, and Upper Ribbon Falls Trails, made improvements at Phantom Ranch, and constructed the transcanyon telephone.

We set up our small tent under the cottonwoods beside Bright Angel Creek. Marguerite Henry's Brighty was named after this stream. A real Brighty lived in the canyon from approximately 1892 until 1922, spending his summers carrying water from a spring below the rim to early tourist accommodations on the North Rim. In the 1970s, wild burros, perhaps Brighty's descendents and the offspring of other burros abandoned by miners in the 1880s and 1890s, threatened the ecological balance of Grand Canyon. The burros roamed freely in the park, eating an enormous amount of vegetation. During my first trip to the Grand Canyon in 1961 I spied a burro perched on a ledge above our camp at Indian Garden. Only later did I discover that something so cute could be so destructive. In 1980 a project to humanely remove the burros from Grand Canyon commenced and eventually five hundred eighty animals were captured and relocated to Texas at a cost of more than $1 million paid for by private donors rather than taxpayers.

Although burros have been removed from the Canyon, other four-legged creatures continued to travel the trails. Mules have been ferrying visitors and freight in and out of the Canyon for over one hundred years. They carried visitors down the Bright Angel Trail to Plateau Point on the Tonto Platform before returning to the rim later the same day. Other visitors rode mules down the Bright Angel Trail to Phantom Ranch and returned to the South Rim via the South Kaibab Trail after their stay in the inner gorge. About 10,000 mule riders enter the Grand Canyon each year. John and I chose to use our own legs to enter and leave the Canyon.

Awakening at dawn on the second morning of our journey, we quickly ate a cold breakfast and headed for Ribbon Falls, leaving my pack and most of our gear suspended high off the ground on metal poles, erected at each campsite to provide a means of protecting packs and their contents from curious or hungry animals. Carrying a light lunch and water in John's small pack, we walked 5.8 miles up the North Kaibab Trail along Bright Angel Creek to the falls. John and I spent nearly an hour lounging by the pool at the base of the falls and showering in the falls before returning to Bright Angel Campground and collecting my undisturbed pack.

Father and son on the trail to Ribbon Falls

We crossed the muddy Colorado on the Silver Bridge and walked west on the River Trail, which joined the Bright Angel Trail at the confluence of Pipe Creek and the Colorado River. The Bright Angel Trail followed Pipe Creek upstream a short distance before the serious business of climbing out of the inner canyon to Indian Garden commenced—the series of switchbacks known as Devils Corkscrew cut in the Vishnu Complex. Above the Devil's Corkscrew the trail traversed through the upper Vishnu layer to the Tapeats Sandstone, through which Garden Creek ran. In this region the Tapeats layer lies directly on top of the Vishnu Schist. The contact between these two layers is called the Great Unconformity because the Grand Canyon Supergroup, the rock layer deposited directly on the Vishnu, eroded away, leaving a 1.25-billion-year gap in geologic time.

Upon reaching Garden Creek John incorrectly surmised that Indian Garden Campground lie nearby. In actuality it was a couple of miles further up the trail. John did not care about the Great Unconformity or any other geologic features of the canyon at that point. He just wanted to be able to stop walking and repeatedly asked me, "How much farther?" I repeatedly answered, "Just a few more steps." He quickly tired of my answer and started to ask, "How many 'Just a few more steps' is it?" I recalled similar sentiments hiking out of the canyon in 1961 but did not have the courage to call out "How much farther?" After nearly seventeen miles of walking since daybreak John was exhausted and had developed a sore foot. He had had enough hiking for one day. I told him his rest would come once we reached the approved campground.

Shadows engulfed a newly constructed Indian Garden Campground upon our arrival. This campground was located several hundred yards upstream from where I had camped in 1961, 1974, and 1989. Now each campsite had a sheltered picnic table and poles with crossbar from which to hang packs. As daylight faded, we pitched our tent and prepared dinner. John stayed awake long enough to take a few bites of a forgettable dehydrated concoction.

Shortly after daybreak we loaded our packs for the final 4.6 miles to the rim. Reinvigorated after a night's rest and foot pain gone, John set a fast pace out of the Canyon—perhaps focused on the dinner he planned to order at El Tovar Hotel that evening. The shared experience of hiking in Grand Canyon with my son was special. I hoped he would want to return with me for another hike in Grand Canyon. When I am dead and gone, will he return to Grand Canyon and feel my presence there? Like the Hopis, I found the Grand Canyon a sacred place and doubt that my spirit could find a better place to return than the Grand Canyon.

Chapter 7
Rick Trujillo

March 1994

No ice, nor frost, nor earthquake, nor volcanic force has left its mark on the canyon.

Ice would have made a lake of it. Frosts would have changed its cliffs to slopes. Earthquakes would have crumbled its walls, and volcanoes would have smeared them with lava. But none of these forces came to mar or help.

In the simplest, easiest and laziest fashion rocks were deposited in the first place. In the simplest, easiest and laziest fashion they have been torn up again, and a view from the canyon rim almost anywhere shows at a glance how it was all done.

—David Starr Jordan (1851-1931), American educator and peace activist, from "The Land of Patience," 1898, reprinted in *The Grand Canyon: Early Impressions*

You either loved Rick Trujillo or you hated him, and once you met him you never forgot him. Not being a reticent kind of guy, he expressed his opinions early and often. It did not take long to form an opinion about

Rick, and Rick quickly decided whether he liked you, and could not care less whether you liked him.

Rick and I became friends in 1966 during our freshman year at Colorado University in Boulder. Rick, the oldest of eleven children, grew up in the little mountain town of Ouray in southwestern Colorado. His father worked in the local mines until failing health forced him to quit. In addition to caring for a large family, his mother cooked for local restaurants during the summer tourist season. Rick started running in grade school in order to see more of the rugged country surrounding his home. He claimed that walking limited the territory he could explore in one day. His running prowess resulted in receiving a cross-country and track scholarship at CU, where he earned All-American honors in cross-country his sophomore year. In the years following graduation from CU with a degree in geology, Rick worked as an exploration geologist in Alaska, the continental United States, Mexico, and South America, but Ouray remained his home. Whenever my travels took me through southwestern Colorado I made it a point to drive through Ouray to visit my old classmate and friend.

Rick was well versed in geology and flora and fauna, capable of incredible physical feats, talkative, incapable of sitting still, opinionated, and intolerant of fools. A confirmed bachelor, he once remarked, "I'd love to have kids, but I'd dislike their mother." His nutritional needs were simple: canned tuna or salmon, raw onions, candy bars, potato chips, cookies, and Mountain Dew or highly sugared iced tea. Despite a high calorie, high sugar diet he remained lean—his arms and legs the caliber and strength of piano wire. He had little use for lazy people, and on a hike rarely altered his pace to allow slower hikers to keep up. Ruth and I hiked with him in the Needles Mountains in Colorado in the summer of 1973. Rick had serious doubts about Ruth's ability to complete the trip, which included climbing to the summit of 14,083-foot Mount Eolus. Once we had successfully returned from our three-day expedition, he paid Ruth his highest compliment, turning to her and saying, "Not bad for a girl."

The San Juan Mountains surrounding Ouray were his playground but he did not limit his adventures to Colorado. Rick has climbed the highest mountain peaks in the northern and southern hemispheres, run mountain races in Europe and the United States, and won the Pike's

Peak Marathon five consecutive years (1973-1977). I have no doubt that Rick could have summitted Mt. Everest but he would not have tolerated the egos or organizational structure of such an expedition.

Rick Trujillo

In March 1994, Rick Trujillo joined Ray Schmidt, my son John, John's friend Ben Alsop, and me for a three-day rim-to-river and back hike via Hermit Trail (U.S.G.S. map: Grand Canyon). This was Ben's initiation to Grand Canyon hiking, while it was John's second and Ray's third trek with me in the Canyon. This South Rim trail started from

Hermit's Rest, which is located at the end of West Rim Drive, eight miles west of Grand Canyon Village. Like many other trails in Grand Canyon, Hermit Trail began as an Indian route. Originally called Horsethief Trail, a prospector, Dan Hogan, began construction of an improved Hermit Trail in 1896.

The Santa Fe Railroad built a road along the West Rim to reach the trailhead and completed improvements in the trail in 1912 and used this trail as an entry into the Canyon in an effort to bypass the one-dollar per mule rider toll that was charged by Ralph Cameron for using the Bright Angel Trail. The Hermit Trail was remarkable for a long section of cobblestone-paved switchbacks, known as the White Zig-Zags, in the Coconino Formation. The railroad named the trail after "the Hermit," Louis Boucher, an eccentric French-Canadian prospector who arrived at the Grand Canyon in approximately 1891 and lived alone at Dripping Springs in an amphitheater of Hermit Basin at the head of Hermit Canyon. The Dripping Springs Trail started 1.6 miles down the Hermit Trail, and Dripping Springs was another mile and a half west. Labeling Boucher a hermit was probably more myth than truth, as he worked as a tourist guide in Grand Canyon. He eventually left the canyon in 1912.

The Santa Fe Railroad also constructed Hermit Camp, a small camp at the end of the trail to provide a stopover for parties headed for the Colorado River, one and a half miles down Hermit Creek. Hermit Camp predated Phantom Ranch by ten years. To supply the camp an aerial tramway was constructed, with the upper terminus at Pima Point. After the National Park Service acquired Bright Angel Trail in 1928, tourist operations were moved closer to the Bright Angel trailhead and Phantom Ranch became the inner canyon destination of choice. Hermit Camp and the tramway were abandoned in 1930 and the structures dismantled; only the foundations of the early tourist camp remain.

Ray, Ben, John, and I flew from Kansas City to Phoenix, rented a car, and drove to Flagstaff to spend the night. It started snowing as we approached Flagstaff, and by the next morning six to eight inches of fresh snow covered the ground. After breakfast and brief forays at backpacking stores in Flagstaff, we drove to the South Rim, which had escaped the snowstorm. Rick drove to the South Rim from his home in

Ouray, meeting us in time for dinner on the evening prior to starting the hike.

Not being a gear freak like me, Rick carried an old, well-used, heavy canvas rucksack stuffed with what he considered basic needs, mainly food. He had little trouble carrying a heavy load for long distances over rough terrain, as long as he had plenty to eat. In contrast to years past, I now sweated every ounce on my back and frequented backpacking stores in Lawrence, Kansas City, Wichita, and Denver in search of that special item missing from my equipment collection and to find lightweight replacements for equipment I already owned. REI catalogues were dog-eared from scrutinizing the pages looking for innovations in backpacking gear.

For this hike I carried my trusty North Face internal-frame pack filled with my lightweight sleeping bag, sleeping pad, a small two-person tent, Nalgene water bottles, Svea stove, fuel, cook pots, bowl and spoon, food, and extra clothes—everything considered essential. Proving my manhood by carrying a heavy pack was not as important as lessening the load on my back.

I attempted to instill my attention to detail in the youngsters, Ben and John, reciting the sage advice preached by Paul Edstrom, my college roommate: "Fail to plan, plan to fail." It seemed I was making an impression on the boys until they met Rick. Paying little attention to either weight, volume, or fashion, Rick quickly stuffed his ancient, dusty rucksack with his sleeping bag, sleeping pad, a six-pack of Mountain Dew, cans of beef stew and salmon, a couple of bags of candy bars, and silverware and a ceramic coffee cup he claimed were on loan from a restaurant he had recently patronized. While it took Rick minutes to ready himself for the trip, it took me an hour. The boys found Rick's method preferable to my time-consuming, detail-oriented method. They had found a new backpacking mentor. Rick had found two attentive students.

As we descended the nearly eight-mile trail from Hermit's Rest (6,640 feet in elevation) to Hermit Camp (3,000 feet in elevation), Rick provided a running commentary regarding the different geological features of the Canyon. The Grand Canyon evolved from an uplifting of the Colorado Plateau and the slicing of the layers of rock contained in this landmass by the erosive powers of the Colorado River and tributary streams. John Wesley Powell compared it to a circular saw spinning in place, as the log it was cutting slowly rose into the blade. The erosive forces of the Colorado River determined the depth of the inner gorge, while running water from rain, snowmelt, and tributary streams were the main erosive forces contributing to the side canyons. Side canyons eroded back into the rims approximately ten times faster than they eroded downward. Because the Colorado Plateau is tilted downhill from north to south, more erosion occurred north of the Colorado River than south of the river and therefore the North Rim is farther back from the river than the South Rim. Erosion has removed eight hundred three cubic miles of rock and contributed to the creation of six hundred tributary canyons. Bright Angel Canyon, Havasu Canyon, and Hermit Creek Canyon were only three of the six hundred side canyons.

Time, wind, and water have exposed an incredible cross section of rocks. During my first several hikes in the Canyon I paid little attention to the geologic strata from rim to river, concentrating on putting one foot in front of the other—the physical challenge of the hike more important than learning about the geology, flora, and fauna of the place in which I hiked. The more I hiked in the Canyon, the more I learned, and wanted to learn, about the different layers of rock. Rick's discourse added to my knowledge.

The rock layers of Grand Canyon record much of the early geologic history of the North American continent. The rocks at Grand Canyon are not unique. Similar rocks are found throughout the world. What is unique is the variety of rocks present, and the clarity with which they are exposed. The oldest layers are on the bottom, the youngest at the top. The youngest layer, the Kaibab Formation, formed two hundred seventy million years ago, is older than the oldest dinosaurs; therefore, no dinosaur fossils are found in the Grand Canyon. The oldest rocks within the Inner Gorge at the bottom of Grand Canyon date to 1.8 billion years ago. The age of the Earth is estimated to be 4.6 billion years, which is somewhat older than the six thousand years professed by many of Powell's contemporaries and a few of mine.

Grand Canyon owes its distinctive stair-step shape to the alternating rock layers in the canyon walls. Each layer responds to erosion differently. Sandstone, limestone, and shale are sedimentary rocks deposited from ancient seas. Sandstone is composed of particles of sand cemented together and is red in color. Limestone is usually white or grey and is created from limy mud and the cemented particles of shells of sea animals. Shale is formed from mud and silt. Hard sandstones and limestones erode as cliffs, while the softer shales between them erode as slopes or shelves, creating the step-sided mesas and buttes that rise like pyramids from the Canyon floor. Hard rocks like schist and granite form narrow gorges such as The Box and much of the inner gorge.

Henry Thoreau said, "The finest workers in stone are not copper or steel tools, but the gentle touches of air and water working at their leisure with a liberal allowance of time." How much time? In contrast to the ancient rocks, the Grand Canyon was created in a relatively short five to six million years and continued to deepen at a rate of one foot every one thousand years.

Trying to remember each layer from top to bottom presents a challenge. The following mnemonic sentence is an easy way to remember the primary rock layers in Grand Canyon: "*Know The Canyon's History, Study Rocks Made By Time Very Slowly*" (*K*aibab Limestone, *T*oroweep Formation, *C*oconino Sandstone, *H*ermit Shale, *S*upai Formation, *R*edwall Limestone, *M*uav Limestone, *B*right Angel Shale, *T*apeats Sandstone, and *V*ishnu Schist). The mnemonic does not account for two layers: the Temple Butte Limestone found intermittently between the Redwall and Muav Limestone, and the Grand Canyon Supergroup.

The Grand Canyon Supergroup is largely sedimentary rock deposited between 1.25 and 1.07 billion years ago. It consists of mudstones, limestones, shales, quartzites, and lava flows. The Supergroup was tilted by faulting, producing the slanted rocks seen today. In many areas an estimated 12,000 feet of rock in the Grand Canyon Supergroup was deposited and then eroded away, creating a gap or unconformity in the geologic record. In these areas the Tapeats layer lies on top of the Vishnu. The missing layer between the Tapeats and the Vishnu is known as the Great Unconformity.

The Vishnu Complex is the oldest and lowest layer in the Canyon. It is comprised of black-colored schist, a metamorphic rock (formed by extreme heat, pressure, and the introduction of new chemical substances), and pink veins of Zoroaster granite, an igneous rock (formed by solidification from a molten state). Remembering the rock layers from rim to river can be difficult despite committing the helpful mnemonic to memory. In my pocket I often carried an illustration of the geologic cross section of the Canyon (see Appendix A).

The Hermit Trail was not maintained by the National Park Service but was reasonably easy to follow, although rockslides obscured the trail several places in the Supai Formation. After a long, gradual downhill traverse through the Supai Formation we stopped for lunch above the Redwall Limestone.

The final 3.8 miles to Hermit Camp, located on the Tonto Platform (Bright Angel Shale), involved descending a series of switchbacks through the Redwall, traversing a gradual downhill grade along the western wall of Cope Butte, and descending more switchbacks through the Muav Limestone to the Tonto Trail coursing through the Bright Angel Shale. Monument Creek, Indian Garden, and the Bright Angel Trail could be reached by walking east on the Tonto Trail, while 1.5 miles to the west lie Hermit Creek and 6.5 miles beyond that an intersection with the Boucher Trail.

Located in a threshold management zone, Hermit Creek Campground boasted a composting toilet and five to six separate campsites. Hermit Creek provided our only source of water (after filtering or purification) for drinking and cooking. Although it was early spring, afternoon temperatures at Hermit Camp pushed ninety degrees, forcing us to seek shelter in the shade of a large rock overhang or to soak in Hermit Creek—a few inches deep and five to six feet wide in most places at this time of year.

On the second day of our three-day hike in the Canyon we walked a mile and a half down Hermit Creek to its union with the muddy Colorado River. Sitting on a huge boulder at river's edge I listened to the roar of Hermit Rapids and watched for rafters. No river runners bounced through the rapids during our brief stay at the river. John and Ben removed footwear and stomped in the wet sand along the river's edge upriver from Hermit Rapids. Before leaving the beach they carved their names in the sand with their toes—a much more ecologically sound endeavor than carving their names on a rock wall.

Back in camp Rick entertained us with his epic stories, including his twenty-seven day traverse of Mount McKinley in 1977—approaching the summit from the southwest by the West Buttress route (Kahiltna Glacier) and descending by the Carsten's Ridge and Muldrow Glacier route. He also shared his adventures searching for precious metals in South America and climbing tall mountains in the Andes. The loads I carried and distances I hiked in Grand Canyon were insignificant compared to what Rick had done.

A full moon rose over the Canyon, illuminating Hermit Camp like a floodlight. I could actually read words on a sheet of paper by moonlight—no need for a flashlight to prepare for bed; however, the bright moon did not interfere with my ability to fall asleep.

We were up before daybreak and on the trail by dawn in order to climb to the rim during the cooler morning hours. As I struggled up the first switchbacks out of camp, Rick, intent on setting a fast pace climbing out of the Canyon, quickly distanced himself from me. Only John stayed with him—Rick's lone geology pupil for the day. Ray, Ben, and I were content with a slower ascent and eventually lost sight of Rick and John.

I elected to walk alone the last half-hour of the climb to the rim, silently reminiscing about my mother, who had died after a brief illness six months earlier. A woman of strong faith, she displayed a youthful zest for life. Despite the arthritis that plagued her during her later years, she did not hesitate to get down on the floor to play with her grandkids or enjoy a walk with my father. When life gave her lemons she made a great lemon meringue pie. An avid reader, my mother instilled in me a love of books and reading. She introduced me to Tony Hillerman, who wrote mystery novels centered in Navajo country to the east of the Canyon, although one of his books, *Skeleton Man*, is set in the Grand Canyon.

My mother never shared with me her thoughts about the Grand Canyon, although she acknowledged my love of the place and gave me a half-dozen books related to the Grand Canyon. She had a fear of heights. I couldn't imagine her standing on the rim peering into its depths. Nevertheless, she appreciated the natural beauty of the earth and shared that love with her children. I was conscious of her spirit in this beautiful place.

Toiling up and down the canyon trails caused one to forget the mundane and trivial matters that often crowded waking hours. It provided a time for spiritual reawakening. A trip to Grand Canyon was more than a geology field trip or exercise in a gigantic gym. It was a place of worship—an immense cathedral with hymns in the wind and a homily in the roiling waters of the river. John Muir was correct—I was connected to all of nature.

The hike to Hermit Creek also allowed me to reacquaint myself with an old friend, Rick Trujillo, and provided an opportunity for Ray, John, and Ben to meet a living legend. I suspect they appreciated his strength, endurance, knowledge, and simple approach to wilderness travel as much as I did.

Leaving my sanctuary, I reached the rim and confronted the cacophony of the outside world. All too quickly my fellow parishioner and friend, Rick Trujillo, bid farewell and headed back to Ouray.

Chapter 8
Heeding Harvey's Advice

May 1995

It is never the same, even from day to day, or even from hour to hour. In the early morning its mood and subjective influences are usually calmer and more full of repose than at other times, but as the sun rises higher the whole scene is so changed that we cannot recall our first impressions. Every passing cloud, every change in the position of the sun, recasts the whole. At sunset the pageant closes amid splendors that seem more than earthly. The direction of the full sunlight, the massing of the shadows, the manner in which the side lights are thrown from the clouds determine these modulations, and the sensitiveness of the picture to the slightest variations in these conditions is very wonderful.

—Clarence Dutton (1841-1912), American geologist

Harvey Butchart was the undisputed king of Grand Canyon hikers. From 1945 to 1976 he taught mathematics at the University of Northern Arizona in Flagstaff, only eighty miles from the South Rim. Shortly after arriving in Flagstaff he discovered the Grand Canyon. His Grand Canyon hiking career spanned forty-two years, beginning in 1945 and ending in 1987. During that period he made five hundred sixty separate hikes, spent 1,025 days in the Canyon, and logged 12,000 miles on various trails and routes, some well known but many discovered by him. Butchart could find no grander place to walk.

Harvey never hiked the length of Grand Canyon in one continuous trip (since the Grand Canyon Enlargement Act of 1975 widely accepted as the two hundred seventy-seven river miles from Lee's Ferry to the Grand Wash Cliffs) but hiked most of its various stages. In 1963 Colin Fletcher was credited with the first below the rim traverse in one continuous walk of the pre-1975 Grand Canyon National Park. The book *The Man Who Walked Through Time* is a narrative of his travels in the Canyon. The week before Fletcher started his journey Harvey became the first man to walk the length of the Park in segments. Colin Fletcher relied heavily on Butchart's knowledge of the Grand Canyon in planning his walk in 1963 and gave Butchart credit for enabling the successful completion of his trip.

In addition to hiking in the Canyon, Harvey wanted to float down the Colorado River on an air mattress without a life preserver. In 1955 he unsuccessfully petitioned the National Park Service to allow him to float from Lee's Ferry to Lake Mead. In early May 1955 William Beer and John Daggett successfully completed an unauthorized swim down the muddy Colorado River from Lee's Ferry to Lake Mead, wearing wetsuits and life jackets and carrying minimal gear. Their trip took twenty-six days. Later that month Butchart and a companion, Boyd Moore, attempted a shorter float down the river starting just upstream from sixty-mile Rapids. This adventure ended in tragedy when Moore was sucked into Lava Canyon Rapids and disappeared.

In four decades of hiking Butchart summitted eighty-three of the named buttes and temples and discovered over one hundred rim-to-river routes within the Canyon. In contrast I have hiked only six rim-to-river routes. Harvey Butchart authored multiple books on hiking in Grand Canyon. He died in 2002 at the age of ninety-five. My love of hiking in Grand Canyon came nowhere near Harvey's obsession with walking in the Canyon.

Joining Harvey Butchart in the pantheon of hiking gods of the Grand Canyon was George Steck. George started hiking in the Grand Canyon in 1957 and during his lifetime hiked approximately 6,000 miles and spent 1,100 days in the canyon. During a six-week trip in

1977 he hiked from Lee's Ferry to Lava Falls and in 1982 spent eighty-two days hiking from Lee's Ferry to the Grand Wash Cliffs.

Steck was enamored with making loop hikes in the Grand Canyon. In 1989 his first book on Grand Canyon hiking, *Loop Hikes in the Grand Canyon I*, was published. He published a second book in 1993, *Loop Hikes in the Grand Canyon II*. In 2002 the two books were combined into *Loop Hikes in the Grand Canyon*. Steck made his last loop hike in the Grand Canyon in 2002 and died on April 13, 2004, at 79 years old.

In January 1995 hometown friends, John Divine, Jerry McKee, and Clay Thompson approached me with the idea of leading them on a hiking trip in the Canyon in May of that year. Somehow they mistook me for Salina's equivalent to Harvey Butchart or George Steck. John, Jerry, and Clay had never hiked in the Canyon but were intrigued by my tales and wanted to experience it for themselves. I was not possessive about the Grand Canyon, and despite my dislike for crowded trails and campsites, I was excited to share my passion for the place with friends. Their appreciation of the Canyon validated mine.

I was the self-appointed leader, travel agent, trail guide, and chief cook and bottle washer—no one protested. Although older than I and a little thicker around the middle, each of my hiking companions was physically fit and ready to take on the challenge posed by a hike in the Canyon. Each of my hiking partners brought a different personality to the group, and fortunately they tolerated my tendency to be impatient and obsessive-compulsive. John Divine—the eternal optimist with a quick smile—greeted everyone with a loud "hello" and upon leave-taking belted out his trademark, "Have a great day!" After a long career at IBM he became a leadership consultant and motivational speaker. Jerry McKee, an early retiree from the Social Security Administration, kept busy by working in his garden, playing golf, and following Kansas State University sporting events. Jerry was Mr. Determination. If he set his sights on a task, he would complete it. Clay Thompson, a retired educator, enjoyed a second career selling real estate. The restless one, Clay had to be doing something. He always arose early in the morning, wondering why the rest of us were not up and ready to join him on the day's adventure.

Originally, I proposed a double traverse of the canyon—hiking from South Rim to North Rim in one day and returning to the South Rim after a day of rest—an incredibly challenging hike I had dreamed about doing for several years and, perhaps, a bit of a reach for an introductory hike for my three friends. Mother Nature interfered with my plans. Heavy spring rains caused flooding in Bright Angel Canyon—especially in the lower aspect of Bright Angel Canyon known as The Box—tearing up the pipeline delivering water from Roaring Springs to the South Rim and washing out a section of the North Kaibab Trail. The park service closed the trail between Phantom Ranch and Cottonwood Campground, making a transcanyon trek impossible.

Similar flooding last occurred in Roaring Springs and Bright Angel Canyons in the spring of 1966, preventing my Scout troop from hiking across the Canyon in June 1966. Having hiked through The Box many times before, I could picture a wall of water scouring the narrow gorge as it raced to the Colorado River. There were places on the trail where it would be difficult to climb out of danger's way.

A rim-to-rim crossing impossible, I decided on a slightly less ambitious trek for my friends—a hike from the South Rim to Colorado River on the South Kaibab Trail and return to the South Rim the same day using the River and Bright Angel Trails. After this introductory hike I suggested we drive to the North Rim and hike down the undamaged upper half of the North Kaibab Trail to Ribbon Falls and back, another sixteen-mile walk in one day. The park service strongly discouraged such long day hikes, posting warnings in visitors guides and on signs at trailheads reading: "Warning: Do not attempt to hike from the rim to the Colorado River and back in one day. Many people who attempt this have suffered serious illness or death." I would never advise Grand Canyon hikers to ignore the park ranger's warnings but stubbornly insisted on making a South Rim to river and back hike and a North Rim to Ribbon Falls and back hike and convinced my buddies they were capable of successfully completing them. Perhaps the gods saw the foolishness of my plans and once again brought heavy rains to the Canyon; mudslides in Roaring Springs Canyon closed the North Kaibab Trail at Supai Tunnel (two miles down the trail), preventing a hike to Ribbon Falls and mandating an alternate North Rim hike. The rains, however, left the South Rim main corridor trails unscathed.

Clay Thompson, Jerry McKee, John Divine, and the author

On a sunny mid-May morning we started our first hike at the South Kaibab trailhead near Yaki Point on the South Rim. The downhill trip went smoothly—an easy walk on fresh legs and with only light daypacks on our backs. Our quartet arrived at the Colorado River by noon, where all were "baptized" in the bone-chilling, blue-green water at the rafter's beach between the suspension bridge and the Bright Angel Creek delta. Since the completion of Glen Canyon Dam (fifteen miles upstream from Lee's Ferry) in 1963, water from deep in Lake Powell traveled through the generators, exiting the dam a cold, nearly forty-eight degrees—it had warmed little by the time it got to Bright Angel Creek. Water from the bottom of Lake Powell warmed up about one degree for every thirty miles it flowed. Before the building of the dam river temperatures approached eighty degrees. After the building of the Glen Canyon Dam Harvey Butchart would have become quickly hypothermic trying to float down the Colorado River straddling an air mattress.

Besides the temperature of the water, the color of the river also changed following completion of the dam. The silt and sediment that gave the Colorado River its classic reddish-brown color before 1963 were trapped behind the dam. Prior to the construction of Glen Canyon

Dam the Colorado River had a maximum estimated flow of 300,000 cubic feet per second and carried as much as 500,000 tons of sediment per day past Bright Angel Creek. After completion of the dam only 40,000 tons of sediment flowed by this point each day. Most of that sediment came from the Paria River, which joined the Colorado River at Lee's Ferry. The Colorado ran blue-green unless the Little Colorado River, its major tributary below Glen Canyon Dam, was running and dumped silt into the water released from Lake Powell.

Flow in the Little Colorado was seasonal, usually running in late winter to early spring. The Little Colorado joined the Colorado approximately 61.5 miles downriver from Lee's Ferry. As a consequence of the change in temperature and silt content of the Colorado River four of eight fish species are extinct and the Canyon's beaver, otter, and muskrat populations have disappeared.

The construction of Glen Canyon Dam also prevented the natural seasonal flooding in the Canyon. Spring flooding, predominately from melting snow in the Rocky Mountains, scoured the river channel, while summer flooding, typically from high-desert thunderstorms, deposited sediment along the shoreline. The elimination of cyclical flooding resulted in loss of sandy beaches along the river. Another effect of the loss of annual flooding was a change in the vegetation along the riverbank, resulting in a change in the insect, bird and animal populations dependent on these plants for cover and food.

With passage of the Grand Canyon Protection Act of 1992 the Bureau of Reclamation was required to implement a plan "to manage Glen Canyon Dam in such a way as to enhance, rather than destroy, the riverside environment downstream." Unfortunately, restoration of cyclical flooding, river sediment, and native fish will require a free-flowing Colorado River—impossible until Glen Canyon Dam is removed.

After a lunch break at the Bright Angel Campground, we proceeded with the uphill leg of the trek on the River and Bright Angel Trails. Near Pipe Creek we passed day hikers in flip-flops and one very fair-skinned young lady who had decided to hike topless, except for her daypack. She sported a severe sunburn from waist to brow. It was amazing how people prepared or failed to prepare for a hike in the Grand Canyon. Hikers wore unsuitable footwear for the rough terrain and failed to protect themselves from the unforgiving desert sun. I have seen families walk several miles down the trail with little more than a quart of water to share. Almost everyone forgot the cardinal rule of Canyon hiking: "What goes down must come up." It may be easy going downhill, but it quickly becomes laborious upon turning around and starting back uphill. The trail always seems steeper and the distance longer on the return trip. Even healthy, well-prepared, intelligent hikers can experience difficulties climbing out of the Canyon, especially on a hot day.

Our group managed to stay together until Indian Garden. At this point, Jerry McKee elected to walk at a slower pace, claiming he would not be far behind us in reaching the rim. On this heavily traveled trail to Grand Canyon Village I had no fear of Jerry becoming lost or getting into trouble and being unable to communicate with us. Besides, he was Mr. Determination.

Clay, John, and I started the final 4.5-mile climb out of the Canyon. Clay and I challenged each other with gradually faster walking speeds. John struggled to keep pace and finished the hike a distant third to Clay and me. During the climb out John neglected to drink an adequate amount of water and upon reaching the rim was suffering from early heat exhaustion. He sought rest and refuge lying motionless on the floor of the art gallery in the Kolb Studio at the head of Bright Angel Trail—a unique addition to the exhibition in the gallery. We would joke about it later, but John's predicament was no laughing matter.

While Clay ministered to John, I retrieved our vehicle at the parking lot at Yaki Point. Upon returning to the trailhead I found Clay and John, but not Jerry. John had recovered after rest and fluids, but Jerry had not been seen. He did not appear to be in distress at Indian Garden, and I wondered what had delayed his climb to the rim. I walked a short distance down the Bright Angel Trail and asked hikers exiting the Canyon if they had passed an older guy with a slight limp and wearing a black elastic knee brace. One or two seemed to recall such a person.

Surmising Jerry must be very slowly making his way to the top, John, Clay, and I decided to check into our motel room before returning to the trailhead to see if he made it out. Imagine our surprise and relief when Jerry greeted us at the motel, grinning from ear to ear and wearing only a towel after a shower. He chided us for being so late and requested clean clothes from the car. Jerry explained that upon reaching Kolb Studio near the trailhead he took a different exit spur, eluding us as we waited just beyond the studio. Since he could not find us on the rim he assumed we had abandoned him, forcing him to walk an extra two miles to our motel room at Yavapai Lodge.

The next morning four very stiff and sore men gingerly piled into a car for the two hundred and fifteen-mile trip to the North Rim. The vehicle reeked of the analgesic balm rubbed into our aching muscles. After sitting nearly motionless for the four-hour trip, standing erect and walking took extraordinary effort. Despite our stiffness and aches and pains we were able to shuffle out to Bright Angel Point, a short distance from Grand Canyon Lodge, and gaze down Bright Angel Canyon and across the canyon to the South Rim, only ten miles away.

The following morning we hiked 3.5 miles along the Ken Patrick Trail (U.S.G.S. maps: Bright Angel Point, Point Imperial) on the North Rim to its junction with the Old Bright Angel Trail. The Old Bright Angel Trail can be followed 7.8 miles from the rim to the junction of Roaring Springs Canyon and Bright Angel Creek, where it intersects the North Kaibab Trail. The Old Bright Angel Trail was seldom used because the North Kaibab Trail down Roaring Springs Canyon provided easier access to the inner canyon.

A heavy overgrowth of scrub oak along the Old Bright Angel Trail scraped our bare legs, causing us to call a halt to our descent after only a half-mile and return to the rim. Upon reaching the rim Clay and I decided to continue on the Ken Patrick Trail for another 6.5 miles to Point Imperial, the highest point on either rim at 8,801 feet in elevation. Jerry and John wanted to return to the car and promised to meet us at Point Imperial in a couple of hours.

Snow covered the Ken Patrick Trail for long stretches beyond the Old Bright Angel trailhead. Clay and I frequently sank knee-deep in the soft snow. Before reaching the Cape Royal Road the trail vanished, or more accurately, we had wandered off the trail. We headed in the direction of road traffic noise. Upon reaching the Cape Royal Road, I made the mistake of turning south (toward Cape Royal) rather than north, where within one hundred yards the trail continuing to Point Imperial could be found. After several miles of walking on the road—the wrong way—it became apparent that something was amiss. The occupants of a car headed in the opposite direction must have noticed our bewildered state and stopped to help us. Embarrassed by my navigational error, I humbly accepted their offer of a ride to Point Imperial, where John and Jerry were patiently waiting.

My friends had done the Canyon—witnessing the beauty and grandeur from the North and South Rims and from below the rim, hiking to its depths and back, shivering in the chilly morning temperatures on the rim and sweating in the furnace-like conditions of the inner canyon, bathing in the Colorado River, inhaling trail dust and the odor of mule urine, and watching the colors of the canyon walls change as the sun made its sojourn from east to west—a truly grand experience. Clay, John, and Jerry understood why I loved this place and joined me as disciples of Harvey Butchart.

Chapter 9
Rim-to-Rim in a Day

September 1996

This Grand Canyon of Arizona is the most stupendous and astounding of all the natural wonders of the earth—and of all earth's natural wonders the latest and the least known. It is a geological apocalypse, half mystery and half revelation.

It is at once the most awful and the most irresistible thing I have ever beheld. It is a paradox of chaos and repose, of gloom and radiance, of immeasurable desolation and enthralling beauty. It is a despair and a joy; a woe and an ecstasy; a requiem and a hallelujah; a world-ruin and a world-glory—everything in antithesis of such titanic sort.

—Fitz-James MacCarthy, "A Rhapsody,"
Grand Canyon of Arizona, 1909

The lights of Kolb Studio loomed above. My mind wandered from the early start to the day on the North Rim to earlier in the century when the Kolb brothers operated a photographic studio at the head of Bright Angel Trail on the South Rim. In 1903 the brothers opened their studio in a tent on the rim and in 1904 built a small two-story frame building nearby that served as their home and studio. One of Ralph Cameron's prospecting holes below the rim became their darkroom.

Ellsworth and Emery Kolb took pictures of parties starting down the Bright Angel Trail on mule back. Notables captured on film by the Kolbs included Theodore Roosevelt, William Howard Taft, William Jennings Bryant, and John Muir. They developed the film, printed the pictures, and sold them to their subjects. The Santa Fe Railroad, competing with the Kolb brothers for the visitor's dollars, refused to provide the Kolbs with clean water to process their photographs. The Kolbs had to descend four and a half miles to Garden Creek in Indian Garden for water to develop their film and hustle back to the rim in time to sell photographs to the returning mule riders. Frequently the nine-mile round trip had to be made twice daily. In 1928 a more reliable source of water became available on the rim, ending the daily dash to and from Indian Garden.

The Kolb brothers were also famous for their trip down the Colorado River in 1911-1912 from Green River, Wyoming, to Needles, California, the first to be recorded on motion picture film. From 1915 to 1976 the movie was shown in an auditorium added to the Kolb's studio on the South Rim. It was the longest running movie of all time. Emery personally narrated the movie until 1948. After 1948 his recorded voice accompanied the film. The evening after completing my 1961 Grand Canyon hike I saw a portion of the Kolb's film.

Ellsworth left the Grand Canyon studio in 1914 and briefly reappeared from time to time until his death in 1960 at the age of eighty-three. Emery continued to live in their home on the rim until his death in 1976 at the age of ninety-five. The building has been restored and houses an art gallery and bookstore. Emery and Ellsworth are buried in the Pioneer Cemetery on the South Rim of Grand Canyon.

The lights of the nearly century-old studio didn't appear to be getting any closer. It seemed as if I was on a treadmill. After walking nearly twenty-three miles, the last half-mile seemed to take an eternity. Earlier that day (September 19, 1996) Jerry McKee, Clay Thompson, and I left the North Rim on a mission to hike across the Canyon in one day, the first half of an attempted double traverse (after a day of rest we planned to walk back to the North Rim in one day). John Divine did not join us for the trip, as he was campaigning (unsuccessfully) for election to the U.S. House of Representatives. He agonized about missing this trip. Had he been able to join us, would he have agonized about the long walk?

Hiking across Grand Canyon in one day is an activity strongly discouraged by National Park Service rangers because of the distance, heat, and steep trails. A traverse of Grand Canyon is the opposite of climbing a mountain—starting downhill when fresh and going uphill when tired. It is imperative that anyone attempting such a feat be in excellent physical condition and adequately trained for a long bone-jarring hike. It is also important to carry plenty of water for the trip and plan for extremes in temperature. It can be near freezing upon leaving the rim in the morning, one hundred degrees in the inner canyon during midday, and chilly once again upon emerging hours later on the opposite rim. Failure to respect the challenges posed by such a trip is a prescription for disaster. Grand Canyon hikers have died attempting shorter distances than a rim-to-rim hike because they overestimated their physical abilities and underestimated the difficulty of the terrain, the effects of the heat, and their need for water.

It is advised that the North Rim be accessible (early May until late October) when such a hike is planned. Dining and lodging facilities on the North Rim are closed from late October until mid-May, and the road from Jacob Lake to the North Rim is closed from late November to May due to heavy snowfall (one hundred fifty inches per year). Also, the hike should be done when daytime temperatures in the inner canyon are cooler (preferably May, late September, or October). Fall is a fabulous time to hike in the Grand Canyon. The temperatures are more moderate and there are fewer people—certainly true this chilly evening, as I was a lone walker on the final traverse through the Kaibab formation to the rim.

Two days earlier Clay, Jerry, and I arrived in Las Vegas on a flight from Kansas City and drove to Zion National Park, where we stopped for the night before proceeding to the North Rim. Before checking in at the Grand Canyon Lodge, I wanted to show Clay and Jerry the Bill Hall trailhead, a starting point for the hike to Thunder River. Just east of Fredonia, Arizona we drove south on a US Forest Service road (FR 422) towards Monument Point. Unknowingly, I turned east on Forest Road 232 to Indian Hollow rather than continue south on FR 422. About a mile down the road, a washout prevented us from proceeding by car. Leaving the car at the side of the road, we started what I thought would be a short jaunt to Monument Point. The short jaunt turned into a four-mile walk. I did not realize my navigational error until reaching the rim and discovering the Thunder River trailhead at Indian Hollow—not the Bill Hall trailhead at Monument Point.

A spectacular view of the Esplanade a thousand feet below made the long walk worthwhile—almost. We turned around and made the long walk back to the car and continued on our way to Grand Canyon Lodge, where we spent the night before starting our hike. Clay had a restless night, spending much of it in the bathroom with diarrhea—a malady he blamed on the Mexican food he ate in Kanab, Utah.

We started down the steep North Kaibab Trail (trailhead at 8,250 feet in elevation) at 5:40 AM—chilly and still dark, but rapidly becoming light. I started my stopwatch. Within an hour we passed through the manmade Supai tunnel (two miles down the trail and 1,450 feet below the trailhead), created by the Civilian Conservation Corps. Twenty minutes later we crossed the bridge across a dry gulch in Roaring Springs Canyon. The bridge was built after a flood in 1966 washed out much of the North Kaibab Trail. Upon reaching the pumping station caretaker's house below Roaring Springs (six-mile mark) Jerry and Clay were already tired and would have turned back had I shared their sentiments. Fortunately, rest, water, and a little food reinvigorated them, and we plodded on, looking forward to easier walking on the relatively level trail along Bright Angel Creek to the Colorado River.

Our path for the next eight miles led through Cottonwood campground, past Ribbon Falls to the west, and through The Box, a narrow portion of Bright Angel Canyon above Phantom Ranch. Only a short climb up Asinine Hill at the Ribbon Falls turnoff interrupted our gradual downhill walk to the Colorado River. We arrived at Bright Angel Campground on the Colorado River at 12:15 PM—covering the first 14.2 miles in seven hours and eleven minutes—negotiating fifty-five switchbacks (forty from trailhead to the bridge in Roaring Springs Canyon, thirteen more to the caretaker's house, and two on Asinine Hill) and crossing six bridges—one across a dry gap in Roaring Springs Canyon, a second across Bright Angel Creek at the junction of Roaring Springs Canyon and Bright Angel Canyon, and four in The Box. In the early 1900s it was necessary to cross Bright Angel Creek ninety-nine times when walking from North Rim to the Colorado River. In 1928 only seven creek crossings were required, but the bridges were more primitive than today's modern structures.

In those fourteen miles we descended through approximately 1.5 billion years of geologic history and four climate or life zones: Canadian, Transition, Upper Sonoran, and Lower Sonoran. The descent from rim to river was equivalent climatically to walking 3,000 miles to the south. Each climate zone we walked through featured plants and animals that were scarce or absent in adjacent zones. The Canadian Zone (an environment similar to the boreal forests of northern Canada) began above 8,200 feet on the Kaibab Plateau of the North Rim and is populated by blue spruce, white fir, Douglas fir trees, quaking aspen, mule deer, Kaibab squirrel, and Steller's jay. The Transition Zone extended from 7,000 to 8,200 feet; ponderosa pine, Gambel oak, and the golden-mantled ground squirrel are among the flora and fauna found here. The fishhook cactus, Utah juniper, piñon pine, blackbush scrub, canyon wren, gray fox, and rock squirrel populated the Upper Sonoran Zone between 4,000 and 6,000 feet on north-facing slopes and 5,000 to 7,000 feet on south-facing slopes. The Lower Sonoran Zone was a hot, dry desert from the Colorado River to approximately 4,000 feet on north-facing slopes and 5,000 feet on southern exposures; it was home to desert scrub (four-winged saltbush and creosote bush), yucca, mesquite, various cacti, pocket mouse, canyon wren, and collared lizards.

Zone boundaries were seldom abrupt; the transition from one zone to the next was gradual and numerous plants and animals typically found in one zone may be found in another. Fremont cottonwoods and a variety of willows grew beside tributary streams. And then, there was the malignant growth of the non-native plant, tamarisk, along the Colorado River.

Tamarisk or saltcedar is a small tree introduced to the southwestern United States a hundred years ago from the eastern Mediterranean to line diversion canals and irrigation ditches to retard erosion. The tamarisk is highly adapted to arid climates, aggressively competes for water with native plants, spreads rapidly via wind-borne seeds, and forms dense thickets along streams and springs unless periodic flooding interrupts its growth and spread. The lack of seasonal flooding of the Colorado River following the building of the Glen Canyon Dam allowed tamarisk to proliferate. The tree can grow in salty soil because it can eliminate excess salt from the tips of its leaves. The salinity of the soil increases when the leaves of the tamarisk fall to the ground, interfering with the growth of native plants and eventually displacing native plants from wetland areas. The leaves, twigs, and seeds of the tamarisk are low in nutritional value and few insects or animals feed on them. The park service is trying to eradicate this foreign invader from the Canyon.

The cold water of Bright Angel Creek felt good on our tired, hot feet. A light lunch boosted our energy for the next nine miles, as we elected to hike out on the Bright Angel Trail. Fortunately, the temperature in the inner canyon was a comfortable eighty-five degrees. Shortly after 1:30 PM Clay, Jerry and I summoned the strength to stand and start the climb to the South Rim, crossed the muddy Colorado River on the Silver Bridge and walked west along the river to Pipe Creek, the start of the uphill hike out of the canyon. The 4.7-mile walk from Bright Angel campground to Indian Garden (3,800 feet) was completed at 4:03 PM (maintaining our two-miles-per-hour pace). I counted another nine switchbacks from the river to Indian Garden, where we took another long break. Shadows were getting longer, air temperature was getting cooler, and I was getting tired.

Only 4.6 miles and forty switchbacks remained. Jerry wanted to rest a few minutes longer at Indian Garden and reassured Clay and I that he would be right behind us. I recalled Jerry saying something similar the last time he was at Indian Garden.

Shadows bathed the canyon. As the sun slowly sank, so did the air temperature—heat was no longer an issue. Clay and I maintained a two miles/hour pace for the next one and a half miles before I hit the wall—my legs failed me. The unexpectedly long walk to Indian Hollow the previous day undoubtedly contributed to my current fatigue. In contrast to earlier in the day, Clay felt much better. I told him to continue at his own speed and, echoing Jerry's words of forty-five minutes earlier, told him, "I'll see you on the rim later." And Jerry—Jerry was somewhere between Indian Garden and me—and he probably did not feel any better than his companions. However, this trip he knew where to meet us—the lobby of the Bright Angel Lodge. He would not attempt to walk to our motel, as it was in the town of Tusayan, outside the bark boundary and approximately eight miles from the trailhead.

By 6:15 PM the sun had set, leaving me in the dark—short of my objective. I focused on the lights of Kolb Studio at the trailhead. Except for the occasional noise of a car on the road beyond the rim, it was eerily quiet. Finally, at 7:12 PM—thirteen hours, thirty-one minutes, and thirty-one seconds after starting the 23.5-mile trans-canyon trek—I reached the top—successfully accomplishing my goal of traversing the Grand Canyon in one day. Clay had finished fifteen to twenty minutes earlier. Amazingly, he felt strong at the finish despite little sleep the night before and the fatigue he experienced during the first few miles of the hike. Jerry made it out nearly an hour and a half later. He was so exhausted he had seriously considered lying down on the trail for the night and hiking out in the morning. After waiting for him for nearly an hour I started yelling "Jerry" into the dark of the canyon. Hearing my calls to him from the rim, he postponed a long rest to make the necessary steps to the top.

Three men from the flatlands of Kansas had crossed the Canyon on foot in one day, although we did not set any records. Harvey Butchart's friend Allyn Cureton of Williams, Arizona, set the single crossing (North Kaibab to South Kaibab Trails) record of 3:06:47 on October 4, 1981, at forty-four years of age. I doubt Cureton walked; he must have run across the Canyon. He also set the double traverse (Kaibab trails) record of 7:51:23 on November 9, 1981. In October 1987 Wally Sheil did a double double-crossing (four trips across the Canyon) in twenty-four hours and forty-five minutes. Elated about crossing the Canyon in a day, we did not care that it took us ten hours longer than Allyn Cureton.

I experienced a mixture of emotions upon completing the walk, including joy, relief, and pride, and understood what Fitz-James MacCarthy meant when he said, "[The Canyon] is a despair and a joy; a woe and an ecstasy; a requiem and a hallelujah," although his statement probably did not refer to walking across the Grand Canyon in one day. I shivered uncontrollably from exhaustion and the chilly evening temperature on the South Rim. Fortunately, a mug of hot chocolate and a roaring fire in the fireplace in the lobby of the Bright Angel Lodge provided needed warmth.

The walk across the Canyon in one day ranked high on my list of demanding physical challenges. Exhausted and satisfied with one crossing of the Canyon in a day, Clay, Jerry, and I huddled and decided against walking back to the North Rim, even after a day's rest. A second trip with only a day of rest seemed foolish—we respected the Canyon too much.

We spent a day on the South Rim behaving as tourists before catching the once-a-day shuttle back to the North Rim. While gazing across the Canyon from the South Rim I overheard a Park Ranger discussing Canyon hiking with a group of visitors. One visitor asked the ranger whether hikers attempted to cross the Grand Canyon in one day. He responded, "Only those fools who want to ruin their knees." I silently agreed that walking across Grand Canyon in one day did not promote joint health, but it was definitely my kind of walk in the park; a dream had been at least partially realized. Another item could be crossed off my bucket list.

Chapter 10
Elizabeth Hikes the Canyon

March 1998

In the Grand Canyon, Arizona has a natural wonder which so far as I know, is in kind absolutely unparalleled throughout the rest of the world. I want to ask you do one thing in connection with it in your own interest and in the interest of the country—to keep this great wonder of nature as it now is. Leave it as it is. I was delighted to learn of the wisdom of the Santa Fe railroad people in deciding not to build their hotel on the brink of the Canyon. I hope you will not have a building of any kind, not a summer cottage, a hotel or anything else, to mar the wonderful grandeur, the sublimity, the great loveliness and beauty of the Canyon. Leave it as it is. You cannot improve on it; not a bit. The ages have been at work on it, and man can only mar it. What you can do is keep it for your children, your children's children and for all who come after you, as one of the great sights which every American, if he can travel at all, should see. We have gotten past the stage, my fellow citizens, when we are to be pardoned if we treat any part of our country as something to be skinned for two or three years for the use of the present generation, whether it be the forest, the water, the scenery. Whatever it is, handle it so that your children's children will get the benefit of it.

—Theodore Roosevelt (1858-1919), speech delivered at Grand Canyon in 1903

President Theodore Roosevelt succeeded in doing more than any other politician to establish conservation as a national policy. When he became president in 1901, there were only five national parks: Yosemite, Yellowstone, Sequoia, General Grant (now part of Sequoia), and Mount Rainer. During his tenure five more national parks and eighteen national monuments (including the Grand Canyon) were added to the list. In addition, one hundred fifty national forests, fifty-one bird refuges, and four national game preserves were created during his tenure—a record future presidents, Republican or Democrat, have been unable to match. The advice to his generation to preserve natural resources for future generations remains timely for our generation.

In the 1880s Senator Benjamin Harrison introduced bills to establish Grand Canyon as a national park. They all failed in Congress because local ranchers, miners, and settlers opposed government intervention in how the land would be used. President Benjamin Harrison placed Grand Canyon under Federal protection as a Forest Preserve in 1893.

Teddy Roosevelt visited Grand Canyon for the first time in 1903. Inspired by its beauty, he remarked, "… to me [Grand Canyon is] the most impressive piece of scenery I have ever looked at." In 1906 Roosevelt signed a bill establishing a Grand Canyon game preserve. A year later the Grand Canyon became part of the Grand Canyon National Forest and in 1908 Teddy Roosevelt established Grand Canyon National Monument. Arizona achieved statehood in 1912 and the National Park Service was created in 1916 to "conserve the scenery and the natural and historic objects and wildlife therein and to provide for the enjoyment of the same in such a manner and by such means as will leave them unimpaired for the enjoyment of future generations." Grand Canyon finally became America's seventeenth national park in 1919, the year of Roosevelt's death.

In 1927 the boundaries of the national park were extended to include more of the Kaibab Plateau. Marble Canyon National Monument was established in 1969, and in 1975 the Grand Canyon Enlargement Act combined Marble Canyon National Monument with the original Grand Canyon National Park to form the current national park extending from the Paria River on the east to the Grand Wash Cliffs to the west. Each year approximately 4.5 million people visit the Grand Canyon, a hundred-fold increase in visitation since designation as a national park in 1919. The Grand Canyon is the second most frequently visited of the fifty-eight national parks in the United States. Only the Great Smoky Mountains National Park in North Carolina and Tennessee attracts more visitors (approximately ten million visitors each year).

Thanks to President Theodore Roosevelt and other conservationists, Grand Canyon has been preserved for my children to enjoy. I introduced my son John to the Grand Canyon just shy of his twelfth birthday. Elizabeth joined me for a trip to Grand Canyon two weeks after her eleventh birthday. We left Salina early on Saturday morning, March 21, 1998, driving to Wichita and catching a flight to Phoenix, where we rented a car and drove to Grand Canyon via Flagstaff, Cameron, and the eastern entrance. I chose this route to show Elizabeth the beauty and wildness of the Navajo Indian Reservation, a sixteen-million-acre reservation that borders the Grand Canyon to the east. Four other modern tribes live in or adjacent to the Grand Canyon. The Havasupai are the only tribe currently living in the Grand Canyon. The Hualapai live south of the western section of the national park. The Southern Paiute reside on the Arizona Strip north of Grand Canyon National Park. The Hopi primarily live in Pueblos on three mesas in northeastern Arizona. The Hopi Reservations are completely surrounded by the Navajo Reservation.

On the afternoon prior to starting our hike we stopped by the Visitors Center to check on the weather forecast and trail conditions. Warm, dry weather was predicted, so we decided to lighten our load by leaving our tent and one camping mattress behind. Leaving the tent behind made sense but I debated the wisdom of taking only one small camping mattress. Lessening the load in my pack won out over comfort in camp. Despite jettisoning the tent and one camping pad, my pack still bulged with my camping gear and much of Elizabeth's stuff. A late addition to our packs was instep crampons purchased at a camping supply store on the rim. A Park Service ranger informed us that the upper segments of the South Rim trails were icy due to packed spring snows and warned us not to attempt a descent into the Canyon without crampons attached to our boots.

On Sunday morning Elizabeth and I took a free shuttle bus from Bright Angel Lodge to the South Kaibab trailhead near Yaki Point. The Park Service no longer allowed hikers to park their vehicles at the South Kaibab trailhead. We started down the trail shortly after 8:30 AM— without crampons on our boots, despite the advice of a park ranger. As forewarned, patches of ice made for treacherous footing the first half mile. Elizabeth slipped on her butt only a few steps from the top. We attached crampons to our boots and cautiously descended through the Kaibab Limestone and Toroweep Formation before removing them.

Once past the ice, we descended at a leisurely pace set by Elizabeth, resting briefly at Cedar Ridge in the Supai Formation prior to negotiating the switchbacks through The Redwall. Elizabeth carried a small internal-frame pack containing her sleeping bag, a jacket, long pants, and water. She did not complain about the load she carried. I cannot say I did not complain about my heavy load. We stopped for lunch at the rim of the inner gorge—a spot just beyond the intersection of the South Kaibab and Tonto Trails called the Tipoff. The slightly downhill grade of the trail across the Tonto Plateau in the Bright Angel Shale gave way to a steeper pitch through the Tapeats Formation, Grand Canyon Supergroup, and Vishnu Complex on its way to the river. We crossed the Kaibab suspension bridge and walked another half mile to Bright Angel Campground, where setting up camp was as simple as spreading out a ground cloth and a sleeping bag and placing our food in large ammo boxes provided by the Park Service to protect it from marauding animals. Our empty packs were suspended from metal poles at our campsite.

Elizabeth waded in the cold water of Bright Angel Creek while I read and snoozed in the shade provided by streamside cottonwoods. John Wesley Powell originally named the stream Silver Creek but later changed its name to Bright Angel Creek, as the clear, cold water of Bright Angel Creek was heavenly compared to the dirty, undrinkable water of Dirty Devil Creek in Utah, an upstream tributary of the Colorado River.

After an early supper we read and watched late-arriving hikers straggle into camp. One of the hikers walking past our camp in the fading light looked familiar. I told Elizabeth, "I think I know that guy."

Elizabeth responded, "Dad, quit staring at him."

"Elizabeth, I think I know that guy," I repeated.

"Dad, you're being rude."

"But Elizabeth, that guy looked familiar," I countered.

Darkness enveloped the inner gorge by 7:30 PM. With little else to do we crawled into our sleeping bags, sharing a single camping mattress placed sideways. I cursed myself for not bringing a second camping pad. Our one mattress provided padding for our heads and upper torsos but not hips and legs. The music of Bright Angel Creek serenaded us as we lie side by side only a few yards from water's edge. I drifted off to sleep wondering whether an old acquaintance had walked by our camp that evening.

Before dawn neighboring campers were awake and noisily preparing for a trip to somewhere else. Their chatter made it impossible to sleep. While walking to the campground bathroom, I encountered the familiar face seen at dusk the previous evening. "Do I know you?" I asked.

"My name is Doug Rollins," he replied.

It suddenly came back to me. Doug and I were both internal medicine residents at KU Medical Center in the mid-1970s. He currently worked as a clinical pharmacologist at the University of Utah in Salt Lake City. It had been seventeen years since I last visited with him during a ski trip to Utah. He, his wife Helen, daughter Emily, and another couple from Salt Lake City had hiked down from the South Rim the previous day. During a leisurely breakfast we exchanged snippets of information about our lives since our last encounter. Doug and his family and friends planned to stay another day at Bright Angel Campground before hiking out. His wife, who had struggled on the hike from the South Rim to the river, fretted about the climb out. She was not the first hiker who realized that climbing out is just as long and more strenuous than the descent into the Canyon.

By mid-morning, Elizabeth and I said good-bye to Doug and Helen, packed our backpacks, vacated our streamside campsite, crossed the Colorado River on the Silver Bridge, and walked along the south bank of the Colorado River to Pipe Creek on the River Trail. Before heading uphill on the Bright Angel Trail to Indian Garden we detoured a short distance down to the Colorado River to allow Elizabeth to symbolically touch the muddy flow—"too thick to drink and too thin to plow." From the river the trail ascended to Indian Garden, zigging and zagging through seven switchbacks in the Vishnu Complex and turning on itself twice more near the Tapeats layer, before reaching Garden Creek. Like my son on his first Canyon hike in 1993, Elizabeth tired of the long walk beside Garden Creek in the Tapeats Narrows below Indian Garden. We briefly stopped in the Indian Garden day use area to rest and eat our lunch before hiking another quarter mile to the campground—silent at this time of day. Hikers were either still on their way down from the South Rim or up from somewhere else. Elizabeth and I whiled away the afternoon hours sitting at the picnic table in the shade of a sheltering roof at our campsite, reading and people watching.

Elizabeth at the muddy Colorado River

After consuming a dinner of half-cooked noodles and crunchy bits of dehydrated meat drowned in a salty brown sauce—a poor imitation of beef stroganoff—we walked out to Plateau Point (3,760 feet in elevation). A guardrail was all that separated us from the Colorado River 1,300 feet below. At least a dozen other hikers joined us in the ritual of watching the sunset over the Canyon from this vantage point. Once the western canyon had gobbled up the sun, Elizabeth and I shuffled back to camp, now a beehive of activity. In the hours since our arrival multiple other hikers had filed into the campground

I cannot remember spending a more miserable night in the Canyon. The cold air, hard ground, and noisy neighbors were not to blame. Some pollinating plant in the vicinity triggered an allergic reaction—my nasal passages were swollen shut and my eyes itched like fury. Unable to breathe comfortably lying down, I spent much of the night sitting at a picnic table with my sleeping bag draped over my shoulders. One benefit of my late night vigil was sky watching. Without the light pollution of civilization I could see an incredible array of stars framed by the canyon walls. On the South Rim, 3,000 feet above me, the lights of the El Tovar Hotel twinkled (despite Teddy Roosevelt's exhortations, the Santa Fe Railroad eventually built a hotel very near the rim).

Before first light I awakened Elizabeth and informed her I wanted to leave Indian Garden as soon as possible. Without complaining she arose and quickly packed her rucksack. As the sun peeked over the eastern edge of the Canyon, we climbed a series of switchbacks in the Redwall known as Jacob's Ladder. At the Three-Mile Resthouse (4,920 feet in elevation) we stopped for twenty minutes to eat a cold breakfast before marching on. Another hour of walking brought us to the Mile-and-a-Half Resthouse (5,720 feet in elevation) and by 9:45 AM we exited the Canyon (trailhead at 6,860 feet in elevation). Patches of ice littered the last mile of the trail but presented no impediment to balance or traction, so we left the crampons in our packs. My allergic symptoms had abated by the time I reached the rim, but after a sleepless night I needed a nap.

Elizabeth did a great job of hiking, and it was a joy to spend time with her in a special place. Her youthful, carefree spirit balanced out the caution and cynicism of my fifty years. She had no problem with the downhill walk of day one but, like her brother John on his first hike in the Canyon, struggled with the uphill hike from the Colorado River to Indian Garden on day two. By the third day she had the hang of Canyon hiking and had no difficulty ascending the final 4.6 miles. She promised to return for another hike in Grand Canyon, but requested better food and her own sleeping pad. We were grateful that Teddy Roosevelt and other environmental visionaries found the Grand Canyon as special as we did.

Elizabeth on the South Rim

Chapter 11
North Kaibab Trail

June 1999

Three features of the canyon strike one at once: its unparalleled magnitude, its architectural forms and suggestions, and its opulence of color effects—a chasm nearly a mile deep and from ten to twenty miles wide, in which Niagara would be only a picture upon your walls, in which pyramids, seen from the rim, would appear only like large tents, and in which the largest of buildings upon the earth would dwindle to insignificant proportions.

—John Burroughs (1837-1921), American naturalist and essayist, from "Temples of the Grand Canyon," 1909, reprinted in *The Grand Canyon: Early Impressions*

My alarm clock rudely awakened me at 3:45 AM on Sunday, June 6, 1999, only three hours after going to bed. Sleep was secondary to making a Grand Canyon hike. My son John and his friend, Ben Alsop, joined the four old men—Clay Thompson, Jerry McKee, John Divine, and me for this short visit to Grand Canyon. There were no novices making the trip this time. By moonlight we loaded our gear and ourselves into Clay's vehicle for the drive to Wichita to catch a flight to Las Vegas. From Las Vegas it was on to the North Rim and a hike down the North Kaibab

Trail, where we would spend two nights at Cottonwood Campground before returning to the North Rim.

We did not start down the trail until mid-morning on Monday because Ben and John wanted to sleep later than the old men. As a token of appreciation for an extra couple of hours of sleep the boys agreed to carry more than their share of the food and cooking utensils to Cottonwood. The old men impatiently waited for the young bucks to awaken, spending the time eating breakfast, organizing gear in backpacks, and gazing over the Canyon rim.

We leisurely descended the North Kaibab Trail on a warm early June morning—the Canyon a riot of color, layers of tan, yellow, and red dotted with green foliage under a brilliant blue sky. Jerry did not casually walk down the trail; he limped down the trail, favoring an arthritic knee. With eleven hours of daylight remaining to make the seven-mile downhill walk to Cottonwood, no one needed to be in a big hurry. Jerry definitely was not. I usually hiked in high-top boots, preferring the ankle and foot support they provided when carrying a heavy pack on an uneven surface. Mistakenly, I left them at home and had to hike in lightweight running shoes. Fortunately for my feet and ankles, my pack was light and the path well maintained.

Near the pumping station caretaker's house below Roaring Springs we stopped for lunch—a great place to halt our ramble because of the presence of potable water. After the break, Ben and my son raced a mile down the trail to Cottonwood Campground and selected a campsite, and then ran back up the trail to see if the older men needed help. Out of pride or stubbornness, or both, none of us yielded our packs to the boys. The afternoon heat slowed our pace, but even Jerry made it from trailhead to Cottonwood in less than five hours.

Dust stuck to our sweaty skin like paint and was scrubbed off in the frigid waters of Bright Angel Creek. The stream was too cold for long soaks, and out of the water it was too hot to do anything but sit in the shade and swap stories and play cards.

The sun finally tucked itself behind the western wall of Bright Angel Canyon about 5:30 PM, bringing some relief from the oppressive afternoon heat (ninety-five degrees). I started cooking supper over the hissing blue flames of small gas stoves. Commencing with this trip I abandoned commercially prepared, lightweight, all-in-one packaged main dishes sold in backpacking stores in favor of meals prepared from ingredients purchased at the local grocery store. This cuisine was cheaper and more flavorful, and often weighed no more than prepackaged dehydrated products. My twenty-five-year old Svea stove continued to function exceptionally well, rapidly heating up a pot of spaghetti sauce—keeping pace with a newer stove used to boil water for pasta.

Our stomachs full and our muscles tired and sore, we had little trouble falling asleep once twilight turned to darkness and stars filled the sky. The canopy of a tent did not impair my ability to see the canopy of the heavens, as tents were left at home.

First light arrived about 4:30 AM and, predictably, Clay could sleep no longer. Accusing him of making no attempt to let his fellow campers sleep, I arose and started water to boil for hot drinks and oatmeal. One by one, the rest of the crew climbed out of their sleeping bags, stretched out the kinks from the previous day's walk and ate a simple meal. John, Ben, Clay, Divine, and I vacated camp by 6:50 AM to walk to the Colorado River and back (a round-trip of 14.6 miles). Jerry stayed in camp, not wanting to put any more miles on his knees before the next day's climb back to the North Rim.

To say we had a brisk morning stroll was an understatement. A faster pace would have required jogging. I felt blessed to be in good enough shape to make a long walk at a fast pace and still enjoy the beauty of the inner canyon, the call of the canyon wrens, and the ever-present melody of Bright Angel Creek tumbling towards the Colorado River. Ben, my son John, and I crossed the Kaibab Suspension Bridge at 9:00 AM, covering over seven miles in just over two hours. Clay and Divine cruised in a half hour later. We snacked and relaxed in Bright Angel Campground and soaked our feet in Bright Angel Creek before starting back towards Cottonwood—at a more relaxed pace, detouring to Ribbon Falls on the trip back. The base of the falls provided a cool, shady spot to rest for a couple of hours before returning to our campsite at Cottonwood. During our absence a scraggly looking wild turkey had taken up residence in our camp and had to be repeatedly chased off the premises.

Ben Alsop and my son John on Kaibab Suspension Bridge

I fixed my signature campout dinner, chicken and noodles with dumplings, to rave reviews. The meal was easily prepared by adding water and canned chicken to packets of chicken noodle soup mix. Dumplings made from biscuit mix were plopped into the boiling mixture, and this comfort food was ready for consumption once the dumplings were cooked.

Darkness fell by 8:30 PM and six tired hikers stretched out on their pads—ready for a bedtime story. Rather than tell a Grand Canyon ghost story, I read aloud from my journal, sharing my memories of previous Grand Canyon trips.

For pure mystery my stories did not match the puzzling disappearance of Bessie and Glen Hyde on a honeymoon float trip down the Colorado River in 1928. No woman had navigated the river prior to the Hyde's attempt. Hoping to earn fame and fortune writing a book and lecturing upon completing their trip through the Grand Canyon, they left Green River, Utah, on September 20, 1928, in a two-ton scow built by Glen. Their boat was loaded with supplies, including a set of bedsprings, but no life preservers. Twenty-six days later they beached their boat at the bottom of Bright Angel Trail and hiked to Grand Canyon Village to purchase additional supplies and visit Emery Kolb.

The couple continued their trip down the river, stopping at Hermit Camp (above River Mile 95) on November 18. They were never seen again, but on December 25 their intact boat containing most of their possessions was found floating in an eddy at River Mile 237. After additional searching, Glen's footprints were discovered near River Mile 217 Rapid, but the honeymooners were never found, and their fate remains a mystery today. Did they fall from their boat and drown? There was evidence that the honeymooners were far from a happy couple. Did one marriage partner murder the other, hide the body, and leave the Canyon? The speculation continues.

Clay once again awakened at first light and started clattering around camp. I arose and started water heating for oatmeal and hot drinks. Clay, John Divine, and Jerry ate a light breakfast, quickly packed and departed camp by 5:33 AM Jerry lightened his load by leaving his sleeping bag, sleeping pad, and ground cloth for my son and Ben to carry. I awakened the boys about 6:00 AM and we left camp within the hour. Despite a nearly eighty-minute head start, I predicted we would pass

Jerry somewhere in the Supai Formation and thought we could catch up with Clay and John Divine before they reached the rim. After two hours of walking, John, Ben, and I passed Jerry on the bridge in the Redwall Limestone in Roaring Springs Canyon. It had taken Jerry nearly three hours to travel this far, and he calculated that he would reach the rim by 1:00 PM. John, Ben and I raced on in hot pursuit of Clay and John Divine, climbing out of the Canyon at a pace I had not matched since my solo climb to the South Rim from Bright Angel Campground on the South Kaibab Trail in 1989. We reached the rim three and a half hours after leaving Cottonwood. Clay and John Divine, who hiked out in just under five hours, reached the trailhead only seconds ahead of the boys and me; I ran past them to touch our parked vehicle first. As I loaded my gear into the van at the trailhead parking lot, a tiny scorpion fell out of a towel tied on my pack and waddled across the pavement. Apparently it had hitched a ride from Cottonwood to the rim. I am not sure the elevation and temperature on the North Rim were conducive to its survival.

While waiting for Jerry to climb out, the five finishers showered in the campground facilities, ate lunch, and checked into our cabin at Grand Canyon Lodge. Shortly before 1:00 PM we drove back to the trailhead and found Jerry waiting for us. He had "topped out" fifteen minutes earlier (hiking out in about seven hours and fifteen minutes).

I asked my adult hiking partners for their thoughts on the trip. John Divine responded, "Interesting experience, but the hike to the river on day two was too much." Jerry said, "My highlight was hiking out in seven hours and fifteen minutes—less than twice the time needed to hike in." Clay commented, "I loved having the boys along." I concurred with Clay, especially when they could carry heavy loads. Several years earlier I had carried a good share of John's gear. Now he returned the favor—carrying his gear, a portion of Jerry's, and more than his allotment of food and cooking equipment. Even more gratifying than having the boys available as beasts of burden was sharing the experience of the hike with my son and Ben. After listening to their adult companions' bad jokes and locker room talk, the boys honored us by calling us teenagers at heart.

Chapter 12
Hermit Creek, Redux

March 2001

My wait was over. The clock read 8:45 AM. If Ruth had not insisted on letting the kids sleep later, I would have been on the trail by 8:00 AM. Waiting this long was painful. John and Elizabeth awakened from their slumber—with a little help from their dad. Before going to breakfast they readied for the hike—emptying their packs, eliminating unnecessary items, and repacking. By late morning we were finally ready and caught the shuttle from Bright Angel Lodge to the trailhead at Hermit's Rest.

John, Elizabeth, Ruth, and I started down the trail shortly after noon on March 22, 2001, an exceptionally late start by my standards. This marked Elizabeth's second hike in Grand Canyon and John's second trip to Hermit Creek and fourth hike in the Canyon. I was making my twelfth trip down into the Canyon—perhaps qualifying me as a serious pilgrim. Returning to the Canyon at regular intervals had become a ritual—a treasured ritual.

Ruth accompanied us for the initial fifteen to twenty minutes of our hike before turning back. A veteran of two previous hikes with me in the Canyon, she remembered the steep descents and ascents and chose not to aggravate pain in her hips and knees on a long walk to the river and back. While Elizabeth, John, and I hiked in the Canyon, Ruth planned to read and relax in her motel room and explore Grand Canyon Village and the Visitors Center on the South Rim.

John and Elizabeth at Hermit Creek Trailhead

I remembered very little of the trail from my first Hermit Creek hike seven years earlier. The trail was quite steep in its upper reaches and poorly maintained in spots, especially along the lengthy traverse through the Supai formation, where several rockslides covered the trail. These rockslides proved more of a nuisance than a challenge to navigation. Elizabeth, now fourteen years old, displayed her characteristic dogged determination by setting the pace, keeping John, a freshman at the University of Kansas in Lawrence, and me behind her. She carried a pack commensurate with her size and age, while John quietly shouldered a pack heavier than mine. We each hauled three liters of water—sufficient for a downhill walk in early spring.

A fast pace for the four miles from the rim to the top of the Redwall contrasted with a slow pace the final 3.8 miles to Hermit Camp—the steep descent through the Redwall and Muav Limestone to the Tonto Platform in the Bright Angel Shale. My legs let me know that they did not appreciate the pounding they received from a downhill walk with me carrying an extra forty pounds on my back. After descending the talus slope in the Muav Limestone below Cope Butte we intersected the Tonto Trail and turned west towards Hermit Creek Campground. On the way to the campground we passed the remnants of Hermit Camp, built by the Santa Fe Railroad nearly a century before. Only foundations of the once-luxury camp remain. It was difficult to imagine that during its heyday between 1911 and 1930, an automobile navigated the rough terrain of Hermit Camp, providing transportation for guests.

It took us five and a half hours to hike 7.8 miles and descend nearly 4,000 vertical feet. I thought we were slow traveling to Hermit Creek, but a Canyon guidebook claimed the hike should take seven hours. A rain shower greeted our arrival at Hermit Creek. In the time it took to extract our jackets from our packs the squall passed. Given our late start, we were the last group of the day to enter a crowded Hermit Creek Campground. Only one campsite was unoccupied; however, it provided a sufficiently large, level place for our tent and a big, waist-high, flat rock to serve as a kitchen counter. John and I pitched the tent, and Elizabeth spread out the pads and bags. Our tent was a tight fit for the kids and me, but did protect us from the elements and mosquitoes.

The sun had set by the time we finished our dinner at 7:00 PM. That evening we put to use one of two new camping products gracing my pack: a headlamp that shed light on the dirty dishes requiring my attention. The second indispensable item added to my collection of gear was a water filter that allowed us to quickly purify water obtained from almost any source.

I awakened about 5:30 AM, a half hour before sunrise. My joints were stiff and my muscles were sore—not unusual for the second day of a Canyon hike. Leaving the kids to sleep a little longer, I abandoned the tent, ate breakfast, filtered water, and wrote in my journal. John and Elizabeth were finally rousted at 8:00 AM. Gnats and mosquitoes pestered us as the kids ate breakfast (I forgot the insect repellant) and readied for a morning stroll to the Colorado River—an easy one-and-a-half-mile walk downstream.

Rock debris flushed down Hermit Canyon and deposited in the Colorado River created Hermit Rapids. The roar of the rapids drowned out all other sounds. I became hypnotized watching the waves and listening to the rumble of the rapids.

The afternoon turned hot, and I rejoiced that the walk back to camp was short. During our foray to the river, Hermit Camp had discharged its many temporary inhabitants, leaving us a choice of campsites. After moving our tent to a larger site, I spent the afternoon resting and reading on a big rock in the shade near Hermit Creek. John and Elizabeth retreated to the tent and read old *New Yorker* magazines carried in by John.

That evening John and Elizabeth helped cook chicken and dumplings—the result not quite to my standards, but edible. We cleaned our dirty dishes as daylight faded and retired to the tent. John and Elizabeth read by the light of flashlights before turning in at the early hour of 7:50 PM. Because we were the only overnight guests at Hermit Camp, the voices of neighboring campers were noticeably absent. Only the flapping of the tent rainfly in the breeze and the murmur of Hermit Creek disturbed the silence.

I awakened at first light and gently prodded the kids to get up and prepare for the hike out. My pack seemed heavier for the outbound trip than for the descent, despite burning the stove fuel and consuming the food I carried into the Canyon. Remembering the prank young boy scouts pulled on Jack McDavid forty years earlier, I accused the kids of putting rocks in my pack.

Afraid that John or Elizabeth's pace would be too brisk for me, I took the lead and set a slow, monotonous pace. We stopped a couple of times for ten to fifteen minutes, otherwise pausing only long enough to take a drink or a photograph or to ask hikers coming down from the rim if they knew how the Kansas University basketball team fared in the NCAA tournament the previous day. One party imparted the bad news—KU lost. Elizabeth and I counted switchbacks—a total of eighty-four for the trip from Hermit Creek Campground to the rim. The previous day we had counted a mere four switchbacks on the trail from Hermit Camp to the Colorado River. It took five hours and thirty-one minutes to hike out, putting us on top shortly after noon. The outbound, uphill trip took no longer than the inbound, downhill trip.

As on my previous climb out of Hermit Creek, I deliberately chose to walk alone the final half mile to the trailhead, enjoying a time of quiet reflection. Seven years earlier I had silently memorialized my mother while walking on this same stretch of trail. This time my attention turned to memories of my father, who had died a month earlier at seventy-eight years of age. I could still remember the prickly feeling of his cheek and the scent of cigarette smoke and Old Spice aftershave when he tucked me into bed and gave me a goodnight kiss fifty years earlier. I recalled how hard he and my mother worked to raise five kids, provide for our education, and support our extracurricular activities. He always encouraged us to do our best without being overbearing. Home was always a warm and loving place.

Neither athletic nor much of a hiker, he nonetheless supported my athletic endeavors. My father did accompany our Scout troop for a hike in Sequoia National Park in 1965, wearing the combat boats and carrying the heavy metal-frame rucksack issued to him in 1943 as a twenty-one year old army recruit destined to serve in the medical corps in Europe during World War II.

I recalled how my dad struggled climbing the last couple of miles to our final destination high in the Sierra Nevada Mountains. Too little exercise and too many cigarettes had him sucking for wind. I hurried ahead, dropped my pack in camp, and hustled back down the trail to help him. He profusely thanked me but the smile on his face when I took his pack was thanks enough. My father taught me the value and satisfaction of hard work and the complementary rule that perseverance pays off—the mantra of the Greatest Generation.

In an episode of the television series *MASH* Major Charles Emerson Winchester III contrasted the distant relationship he had with his father with the close relationship Hawkeye had with his father. "I had a father," Charles stated, "You had a dad." I also had a dad. With a lump in my throat I reached the rim, joining John and Elizabeth for the bus ride from Hermit's Rest to Grand Canyon Village and a reunion with Ruth.

Chapter 13
Return to Thunder River

October 2002

Having an adventure shows that someone is incompetent, that something has gone wrong. An adventure is interesting enough in retrospect, especially to the person who didn't have it; at the time it happens it usually constitutes an exceedingly disagreeable experience.

—Vilhjalnus Stefanoson (1879-1962),
My Life with the Eskimo

Upon awakening the first morning below the rim I was greeted by a weary-looking Clay Thompson. True to form Clay had arisen before anyone else and was packed up and ready to go—albeit in the opposite direction than originally planned. He wanted to quit the trek after one day on the trail, claiming that if he continued the descent into the Canyon he doubted his ability to climb out. Had I grossly underestimated Clay's mental and physical toughness? I was dumbfounded by his pronouncement to quit prematurely. A plan to salvage the trip had to be made in a matter of minutes.

During John Wesley Powell's first expedition down the Colorado River in 1869, William Dunn and the Howland brothers, Seneca and O. G., decided to abandon the trip after nearly three months on the river. The three men feared they would die if they continued down the river. After leaving Powell they hiked out to the Arizona Strip on the north side of Grand Canyon where they were eventually killed. The person or persons responsible for their deaths remains a mystery. Powell would complete the historic trip through the Grand Canyon two days after the confrontation with three crewmembers at what is now known as Separation Canyon. The peril facing Clay certainly did not compare to that of Dunn and the Howland brothers, as Clay did not fear for his own life. Nevertheless, his decision threw a wrench into the works.

Six months earlier Clay and John Divine had petitioned me to lead another expedition in Grand Canyon. Because of bad knees Jerry McKee had retired from hiking. I wanted to repeat the Thunder River hike of eleven years earlier, and warned Clay and John that this trip would be longer and rougher than any hike they had previously completed. In contrast to the main corridor trails, the trails to Thunder River were very steep and poorly maintained in places. Emergency medical care, if needed, would be difficult to obtain. John and Clay were not dissuaded. We invited another Salinan, Lee Young, to hike with us, and added a fifth, my old college friend, legendary mountain runner, and occasional Canyon hiker, Rick Trujillo, still living in Ouray, Colorado. He remained the iconic high country hiker.

In 1995 Rick and a fellow mountain runner, Ricky Denesik, climbed all fifty-four of the 14,000-foot peaks in Colorado in record time (fifteen days, nine hours, and fifty-five minutes). In less than sixteen days he and his hiking companion walked three hundred thirty-seven horizontal miles and climbed 156,130 vertical feet. If that wasn't enough, in 1996, at the ripe old age of forty-eight, Rick won the Hardrock Hundred Endurance Race, a 101.7 mile loop through the San Juan Mountains starting and ending at Silverton, Colorado, and passing through Telluride and Ouray. He completed the race in thirty hours, forty-four minutes, and seventeen seconds. I doubted that this Canyon trip would tax Rick too much.

We drove from Salina to Grand Canyon, picking up Rick in Grand Junction, Colorado, and arrived at the Bill Hall trailhead at Monument Point on the North Rim on Monday morning, October 7, 2002. It was a half-mile walk along the rim from the parking lot at road's end to the trailhead at Monument Point (7,200 feet in elevation). The vegetation along the rim had not recovered from a 1996 fire that charred thousands of acres of forest and woodlands on the western reaches of the Kaibab Plateau along the North Rim. Rick led the way with his characteristic bouncing gait, more kangaroo than human. He still carried an old rucksack containing his favorite foods to supplement the meals I planned. In contrast to my trip to Thunder River in 1991, we had no trouble finding the location where the Bill Hall Trail (named after a seasonal park ranger killed in 1979 in an automobile accident) plummeted off the rim.

The upper segment of the trail was exactly as I remembered it, steep and strewn with loose rocks. Clay complained of rubbery legs within the first mile, a foreshadowing of events to come. We hiked about two hours before stopping for lunch. John and Clay were duly impressed with the difficult descent, especially one particularly imposing drop-off in the Coconino Formation, affectionately referred to as "The Cliff," which required removal of our packs and carefully backing down the slope on all fours. Packs were lowered by rope from the top of the ledge to the trail below.

Upon reaching the Esplanade the trail leveled and the temperature rose. Water for use on the return trip was cached at two separate places on the Esplanade. Rick Trujillo carried a GPS and recorded the exact location of the hidden gallon jugs of water. We walked across the pink rock of the broad, nearly level Esplanade to the edge of the Redwall, where forward progress halted for the night. Surprise Valley could be surveyed 1,000 vertical feet below. Clay rolled out his sleeping pad, assumed a supine position, and moved very little the remainder of the evening. He said nothing about wanting to turn back. I assumed that dinner and a good night's rest would restore his energy and spirit.

Early on the morning of the second day of the trip Clay made his announcement. He would not proceed, but did not want to ruin the hike for the rest of us. He unilaterally decided to hike out by himself and insisted that we continue without him. I respected Clay's assessment of his abilities and did not attempt to dissuade him from turning back; however, Clay's decision violated a rule agreed upon before starting the hike: No one would hike alone on this wilderness trip. Especially Clay, who had no sense of direction.

After a brief discussion, John Divine volunteered to hike out with Clay. They planned to return to the van—a six-mile walk—find a motel room in a nearby town, and return for us at the Monument Point trailhead in three days. I was disappointed that Clay and John would not continue as originally proposed, but could not immediately develop a better plan. Recalling Glenda Schmidt's mishap in 1991, I wondered if every Thunder River trip would be plagued by trouble on the trail, and then I remembered that this was my thirteenth hike in the Canyon—a little bad luck had to come my way.

Before departing, Clay and John left us the food, fuel, stoves, and cooking utensils they had been carrying. Rick, Lee, and I decided to lighten our loads by caching excess food and Rick's tent in a rock crevice near our first night's camp. We would retrieve these items on the return trip. John and Clay headed north across the Esplanade, while Rick, Lee, and I headed south—clambering down multiple switchbacks through the Redwall to Surprise Valley (3,800 feet in elevation), walking west across Surprise Valley, and descending another 1,400 vertical feet to Deer Creek. In 1991 Ruth and I traveled in a clockwise direction from Surprise Valley—hiking east to Tapeats Creek, south along the creek, west along the Colorado River, and north along Deer Creek to Surprise Valley. This time we followed a counterclockwise route—west out of Surprise Valley to the Deer Creek drainage, south to the Colorado River, east along the river, up Tapeats Creek Canyon, and back to Surprise Valley.

It took us nearly four hours to descend from our camp on the Esplanade to Deer Creek. Already tired and sore from the previous day's jarring downhill jaunt, the second day's descent compounded our misery. I wondered how Clay and John were doing. I had no doubts that they could make it out safely but it was unsettling not knowing where they were. Upon reaching Deer Creek, we ate lunch and replenished our nearly depleted water stores, filtering fifteen liters of water for the next leg of the trek. We hiked about a half mile along the west bank of Deer Creek and before reaching Deer Creek Narrows we sloshed across the shallow stream to a trail on the opposite bank and climbed to a saddle in a steep slope to the southeast. The view from the saddle was breathtaking—six hundred feet below us the Colorado River flowed through the Granite Narrows. In the mid-afternoon sun the river was a shimmering ribbon of silver bisecting sheer granite cliffs.

Walking east, high above the river, we zigzagged in and out of small drainages on a dusty path that I later learned was called the Granite Narrows Trail. There was absolutely no shade on this trail and the afternoon temperature must have been in the nineties. The walk above the river seemed interminably long, an estimated three miles between the saddle and a final descent to the bank of the Colorado River. Dog-tired from the physical demands of the first two days of the journey, Lee and I voted to call it quits for the day upon reaching the river. Even old mountain man Rick welcomed a break.

We had originally planned to spend the night in a campground on lower Tapeats Creek, another mile upriver. With daylight fading and our energy ebbing, we decided to proceed no farther and made camp on a small beach on the river just below Hundred and Thirty Five Mile Rapids.

Lee attempted to filter water from the murky Colorado, managing to produce only a couple of liters of clear liquid before the silt in the river water plugged the pores of the ceramic filter. We managed to survive with what he filtered and the several liters remaining from the fifteen liters we carried after leaving Deer Creek five hours earlier. We rolled our sleeping bags out on dry sand ten yards from the rumbling river's edge. Sleep came quickly despite the river's roar.

Rick, Lee, and I were up at dawn of day three, anxious to procure fresh, clear water at Tapeats Creek rather than drink the silt-laden water from the river. We decided to postpone breakfast until we reached Tapeats Creek. Hiking east along the Colorado River, we crossed Bonita Creek drainage and climbed over a granite outcropping before descending to the beach and hiking another half mile to Tapeats Creek. It took an hour to hike from our riverside camp to the confluence of Tapeats Creek and the Colorado River. Upon arrival at Tapeats Creek I attempted to resurrect my water filter, but all efforts failed. A piece of the one-way valve mechanism had gone missing while trying to clean the filter. We would have to treat water (iodine tablets), boil it, or use the Rick Trujillo method—drink it untreated (and hope that it wasn't tainted). Pancakes were on the breakfast menu—a departure from the usual fare—but finding only the syrup mix, oatmeal had to do. John or Clay must have escaped with the pancake mix. After breakfast we pressed on towards Upper Tapeats Campground, three miles upstream and four hundred forty feet higher in elevation.

From the beach on the Colorado River (2,000 feet in elevation) the trail climbed a steep talus slope to the west of Tapeats Creek to bypass the deep lower gorge. Shortly after completing this climb we stumbled upon a Grand Canyon rattlesnake—the only snake endemic to the Canyon and the only rattlesnake commonly found in it. Harvey Butchart estimated he saw one rattlesnake for every forty days spent in the Canyon. This was the first rattlesnake I observed in forty-eight days in the Canyon. The snake, coiled in a rock crevice to the side of the trail, was preoccupied with swallowing a mouse it must have just caught. The mouse's tail and rump protruded from the snake's mouth. Leaving the snake to finish its meal, our walk continued on level ground, now high above Tapeats Creek in the chasm to our right.

The trail eventually intersected the creek and we cautiously waded across the swiftly-moving, knee-high water to the east bank of Tapeats Creek and continued upstream for two miles before making a final crossing to Upper Tapeats Campground on the west bank. Arriving in camp by mid-afternoon, we rehydrated, rested, and attempted to stay out of the hot afternoon sun.

Out of laziness I abandoned my plan to make chicken and noodles with dumplings in favor of chicken noodle soup, complemented by tabouli and berry cobbler. The night turned chilly and Lee loaned me the rainfly from his tent, which I wrapped around my lightweight sleeping bag for added warmth.

Thursday morning I awakened before dawn to start heating water. After a quick meal we loaded our packs and headed uphill to Thunder Springs (3,400 feet in elevation), a one-hour hike along the cascading Thunder River. At Thunder Springs water poured out of the side of a canyon wall from many portals, nourishing an abundance of streamside vegetation. We filled all of our water containers, as there were no water sources the remainder of the journey, except for our cached gallon jugs. I prayed they remained undisturbed where concealed along the trail.

As much as we would have liked to spend a few hours resting at this oasis, our plan called for a traverse of the Esplanade before dusk. We climbed into Surprise Valley and hiked one and a half miles west across the valley floor to the junction with the spur to Deer Creek. The loop completed, we turned north and retraced our steps up the Redwall to the Esplanade, recovering items cached near our campsite of three days earlier. During our two-and-a-half-day absence, some animal had discovered Rick's stash of peanut butter, managing to open the container's lid, and lick the jar clean. After a long rest in the shade of a rock overhang on the Esplanade our journey continued northward another three and a half miles before making camp at the same site Ray, Glenda, Ruth, and I camped on the first night of my first trip to Thunder River eleven years earlier.

Scattered around the campsite on the Esplanade were multiple strange-looking patches of earth, accurately described by one Canyon journalist as having the appearance and consistency of crushed charcoal. I had never noticed this soil before, although it is commonly found along Grand Canyon trails, especially on the Esplanade. They were clumps of cryptogamic soil and consisted of flowerless or seedless plants that reproduced by spores (such as fungi or mosses). This soil forms a protective crust against wind and water erosion and absorbs and retains moisture, promoting growth of larger plants. Hikers are implored to avoid walking on this living soil, as, once disturbed, it may take twenty-five years or more to redevelop.

After a dinner of red beans, rice, and cornbread, we watched, videotaped, and photographed a magnificent sunset over the Esplanade. My cooking was good—the after dinner show was even better. The sunset rivaled any sunset I had previously observed in the Canyon. The setting sun surrendered to the glow of lights from Las Vegas. The neon glitz of Las Vegas was no match for a Grand Canyon sunset.

Our routine continued—to bed at sundown and up at dawn. We were on the trail by 7:37 AM of day five. Rick, Lee, and I felt chipper after four days of hiking, making quick work of the final three miles to the rim, cautiously scaling "The Cliff" without removing our packs. Lee's only comment upon completing the hike was, "I'm pooped." Rick added, "The Grand Canyon is grand." I agreed with both of them. It had been a long and physically demanding hike in one of the most beautiful areas in Grand Canyon.

Lee Young on the Bill Hall Trail

After an easy half-mile jaunt along the rim we reached the parking lot, hoping to find Clay and John waiting for us—no such luck. However, my anxiety over Clay and John soon abated, as shortly after Lee, Rick, and I jettisoned our packs and sorted through our gear, they drove up in the van. In the three days since last seeing Clay and John I had thought of an alternate solution to their turning back. Clay and John could have hiked several miles down to Upper Tapeats Campground, a mile beyond Thunder Springs, where they could have rested for two days while Lee, Rick, and I hiked down the Deer Creek drainage, along the

Colorado River, and up Tapeats Creek. I regretted that Clay and John were unable to finish one of the premier hikes in Grand Canyon but rejoiced that they made it out of the Canyon safely—and had returned for Rick, Lee, and me!

Chapter 14
A Guy Thing

May 2004

You cannot see the Grand Canyon in one view, as if it were a changeless spectacle from which a curtain might be lifted, but to see it you have to toil ... through its labyrinths.

—John Wesley Powell (1834-1902),
The Exploration of the Colorado River and Its Canyons

Major John Wesley Powell, a one-armed Civil War veteran, is probably the greatest single figure in the history of the Grand Canyon and the Colorado River. He is best known for leading an expedition of nine men in four small wooden boats down the uncharted Colorado River through the Grand Canyon from May 24 until August 30, 1869. One man abandoned the trip after the first month and three others quit only three days before the expedition reached the Virgin River, Powell's final destination. The three men calling it quits at Separation Canyon were presumed killed after reaching the rim by the Shivitz band of the Northern Paiute Indians. However, one historian claims the three men were killed by Mormon settlers on the North Rim who mistook them for federal agents searching for John D. Lee, the accused ringleader of the 1857 Mountain Meadows Massacre in which one hundred twenty non-Mormons bound for California were murdered.

Major Powell led a second expedition down the Colorado River in 1871. It was on this trip that he named the canyon through which he traveled the Grand Canyon. In 1881, he assumed the directorship of the U.S. Geological Survey, a position he held for thirteen years. Powell recognized that water, or the lack of it, would be a major obstacle in America's westward expansion. In 1883 in a speech given at the First International Irrigation Congress in Los Angeles Powell argued, "There is not enough water to supply the land." He favored organizing settlements around water and watersheds, which would force water conservation, a policy ridiculed by developers of his day and largely ignored today. In his book *Grand Canyon-River at Risk*, Wade Davis, an Explorer in Residence at the National Geographic Society, noted that more water is exported from the Colorado River than any other river basin in the world; the economy of the American Southwest is dependent upon the river.

It is ironic that the original grandeur of Glen Canyon and the seasonal variation in water flow through the Grand Canyon were irreparably altered by the construction of Glen Canyon Dam and the creation of the lake that bears Powell's name. The wild river navigated by Powell and his men can still be wild but the fluctuations in river volume, once natural, are largely dependent on the power needs of the southwest. Robert F. Kennedy, Jr., chairman of Waterkeeper Alliance, an international organization defending local waterways from polluters, lamented that production of hydroelectric power has taken precedence over managing the river as a national park. In his introduction to Edward Abbey's classic novel, *The Monkey Wrench Gang*, American author and historian Douglas Brinkley was just as brutal in his criticism of Glen Canyon Dam, calling it "a pork-barrel project" built to provide low cost energy to Los Angeles, Las Vegas, and Phoenix.

In the fall of 2003 John Divine approached me about leading a hike in Grand Canyon in early May 2004. The presence of Glen Canyon Dam did not dampen his enthusiasm for another walk in the park. He was once again ready to toil through its labyrinths. Why was John always the alleged instigator of these hikes? Ready for another pilgrimage to the Canyon, I needed very little encouragement to start planning. It had been over a year since my last trip to the Canyon, and I was ready for the figurative battery recharge provided by a trek below the rim.

My plans were temporarily derailed in December when I ruptured a disc in my back. Fortunately, my back pain resolved with a program of physical therapy and my physician gave me permission to proceed with a Canyon hike.

Because the visitor's facilities on the North Rim would still be officially closed in early May, I narrowed our options to South Rim hikes and finally decided on a hike to Hermit Creek. Although I had hiked to Hermit Creek twice before, my hiking companions had never been there and it offered a challenging alternative to hiking the main corridor trails. In addition to John Divine, four other souls joined me for the hike: Clay Thompson, John Mize (my friend and lawyer), Dirk Hutchinson (a fellow physician in Salina), and Tim Holm (a friend of John Divine's from Abilene, Kansas). Clay's enthusiasm for another Canyon hike was not dampened by his difficulties on the trail to Thunder River in October 2002.

We were on the trail by 9:00 AM on May 15, 2004. Comfortable temperatures greeted the commencement of our hike—shorts and short-sleeve shirt weather. We each carried four to five quarts of water for the nearly eight-mile journey. Although Santa Maria Spring is located two miles down the trail, the water running from the spring is only a trickle; replenishing our water supplies there would take hours.

The Park Service did not maintain Hermit Trail and it seemed in worse shape than I remembered from previous trips. At irregular intervals rockslides obscured the trail as it coursed through the Supai formation, causing us to pick our way over or around the obstruction. After three hours of walking we reached Lookout Point at the brink of the Redwall—a level place to eat lunch with a great view of the inner gorge. After this break we descended through the Redwall to the Tonto Platform. There was no shade from the top of the Redwall to the camp at Hermit Creek, and temperatures near the century mark sapped what little energy we had left.

I asked John Mize if he had thought about his job in Salina at any time on the walk down the trail. "Not a bit," he responded. Like me, he had been concentrating on the rigors of the hike and the beauty of the surroundings.

We reached Hermit Creek Campground at 3:45 PM—a six hour and forty-five minute trek—over an hour longer than it took Elizabeth, John and I to make the same distance three years previously. Undoubtedly, our ages and the heat contributed to the slower pace this trip. During the downhill journey to Hermit Campground John Mize developed a painful blood blister under the toenail of the great toe of his left foot, and he limped the final mile to camp. Fortunately, our designated trip physician, Dirk Hutchinson, skillfully attended to John's ailment.

Tents were pitched at a site a short distance from Hermit Creek. Clay immediately filtered nearly three gallons of water for drinking and cooking, using a new water filter I purchased to replace the one irreparably damaged on the Thunder River trip in October 2002. As usual, I cooked dinner (chicken fajitas with real onions, bell peppers, and cheese) for the group and supervised the cleanup process.

Darkness enveloped camp by 7:45 PM and we were all in bed shortly thereafter. I shared space in my tent with Tim Holm. Clear skies were predicted for the entire trip, so I left the tent's rainfly in the car at the trailhead. The tent provided shelter from the insects but hindered stargazing. Unfortunately, my camping mattress would not stay inflated. Trying not to disturb Tim, I rolled off the mat, inflated it by blowing air into the valve, and rolled back on it, only to have it deflate within minutes. After several more attempts I gave up and spent a restless night lying on hard ground—reminiscent of my first trip to Grand Canyon.

By 5:00 AM it was light and I started the stoves to boil water for our traditional breakfast fare—oatmeal and hot tea, coffee and cocoa. Shortly after 7:00 AM, we left camp for the short walk to the Colorado River. The river can be approached by simply walking beside and, often, in Hermit Creek. It can also be reached by climbing up to Hermit Trail on the Tonto Plateau above Hermit Campground, following the trail north several hundred yards before descending west to rejoin Hermit Creek, and walking the trail beside the creek to the river. We chose the latter route first.

I wore sandals for the short hike, walking in the shallow waters of Hermit Creek much of the way. The group spent an hour on the shore of the emerald-colored Colorado River, and while there observed a couple of rafts negotiate Hermit Rapids. Hermit Rapids was one of one hundred sixty named rapids commercial rafters negotiate between their starting point at Lee's Ferry and taking out two hundred twenty-six miles downriver at Diamond Creek. Fifty-six of the rapids were rated

113

serious, yet Wade Davis claims that riding a raft down the Colorado River is safer than riding a bicycle through the streets of New York City. Since Powell's perilous trip down the Colorado River in 1869, hundreds of thousands of people have safely made the journey.

Tim Holm, Clay Thompson, Dirk Hutchinson, and John Divine at Hermit Rapids

We decided to follow Hermit Creek the entire way back to Hermit Campground, rather than retrace our outbound route and, unknowingly, walked beyond our campsite. Fortunately, someone looked back and saw tents on the opposite side of the stream—our tents! Upon returning to our campsite I discovered that something, presumably a rodent, had chewed a mouse-sized hole through the backpack I had loaned Tim for the trip. Although he had removed all food from the pack prior to laying it on the ground there must have been some residue that attracted the pest. Now I possessed two packs gnawed on by Canyon wildlife.

The afternoon temperature soared to a hundred five degrees, forcing us to keep cool by lying in the shade or soaking in shallow pools of Hermit Creek, where minnows nipped at our exposed skin. Once the shadows started to lengthen our lethargy lifted and dinner was prepared—Clay's favorite camp meal and my speciality, chicken and dumplings.

Tim Holm in Hermit Creek

After dinner we sat around camp—sans campfire—swapping stories of our most demanding physical endeavors. Dirk recalled shoveling wheat from railroad cars in the heat of summer. Clay shared his experience extracting grain samples from railroad cars during an equally hot summer. John Divine remembered working ten- to twelve-hour days constructing forms and pouring concrete during a summer between college semesters. Crossing the Canyon in one day in 1996, my hike to Thunder River in 2002, and five-mile ocean swims from Buck Island to St. Croix in the Caribbean in 2001 and 2003 ranked high on my list of physically challenging activities. Somehow, John Mize's recollections went unrecorded—just like a lawyer to be off the record! I suspect our discussion was a guy thing, like rams butting heads to determine the strongest. I could not envision my wife sitting around with a group of women friends sharing stories of the physical challenges they faced at work or play.

Being creatures of habit, as well as old and tired, we were in bed shortly after 8:00 PM. It was a quiet and warm night, although perhaps slightly cooler than the previous night. Able to repair a tear in my mattress, I slept more comfortably. Tim Holm abandoned the tent in favor of sleeping under the stars on a large, flat rock near our campsite. Did he fear I would wrestle with my sleeping pad again or did he dislike my snoring?

Monday morning our party awakened at 4:30 AM and by the light of headlamps ate breakfast and broke camp. As recommended for spring, summer, and early fall hikes, we wanted to be out of the inner canyon before it became too hot. We were on the trail before official sunrise and scaled the Cathedral Stairs switchbacks through a break in the Redwall before taking our first rest. After two hours of walking the long traverse in the Supai Group we reached Santa Maria Springs and took a second break at the large, wild-grape-covered resthouse located there.

Once sufficiently rested and hydrated, we began the long, steady two-mile climb through the final four layers to the top: Hermit Shale, Coconino Sandstone with its cobblestone path, Toroweep Formation, and the Kaibab Limestone. I took the lead after Santa Maria Springs and loudly announced that I would not stop until someone literally cried "uncle." I pushed the pace a little, testing the mettle of my companions. No one spoke up and no one stopped. Five hours and fifty minutes after leaving Hermit Camp our troop emerged from the Canyon—nearly one hour faster than the trip down two days earlier, and only twenty minutes longer than it took Elizabeth, John, and I to hike out three years previously. Clay, who twenty-four hours earlier had expressed apprehension about the eight-mile uphill trek from Hermit Camp to the rim, had no trouble hiking out. The demon of Thunder River had been exorcised.

I started using a hiking staff during my trip to Thunder River in 1991. I firmly believe that using a walking stick going downhill took some of the stress off my knees, especially when carrying a heavy pack. It also helped with balance on steep, uneven terrain and when crossing streams. This trip I traded my single hiking staff for two trekking poles and had absolutely no problems with knee pain. I was sold on trekking poles.

I queried each of my hiking companions about their experience. Dirk said, "Great trip … the hardest physical thing I've done in my life … harder than shoveling wheat out of a railroad car." John Divine said, "Great experience … I was still having fun at the end." Clay added, "The chef provided outstanding meals … chicken and noodles his supreme accomplishment." Tim remarked, "An amazing trip … enjoyed the company … inspired by the old geezers (Clay and John Divine)." John Mize somehow managed to avoid the interrogation. I concluded that this trip proved more difficult for me than my two previous trips to Hermit Creek—perhaps a sign of my aging. Nevertheless, I still loved the physical challenge of the hike, the camaraderie of my hiking companions, the temporary escape from my usual daily routine, and the natural beauty of the Canyon.

Chapter 15
R2R2R#3

May 2006

saunter: (son'ter), intransitive verb. To stroll.

—*The American Heritage College Dictionary,*
Third edition

I awakened early on the morning of May 27, 2006, not sure I could get out of bed. My calves felt like they had been beaten with a baseball bat. Movement triggered sharp pain in my sacroiliac region and right knee. My son John and his friend, Benji, remained asleep in an adjacent bed in our motel room on the South Rim. Not wanting to awaken them, I refrained from howling. Once on my feet I discovered I could walk, but my initial steps were very tentative. My first task was to get to the bathroom. A return hike to the North Rim was not on my "To Do" list yet. Once in the bathroom I took two ibuprofen and filled the tub with hot water and slipped in for a long soak. The hot water soothed my aching muscles. Feeling better, I reassured myself that I could walk across the Canyon again—but not in the next twenty-four hours. I needed a day of rest.

In November 2005 my son approached me about a rim-to-rim-to-rim (R2R2R) hike in the Grand Canyon. He and a couple of his college friends were interested in walking across the Grand Canyon in one day and hiking back after a day of rest. John wondered if I would be interested in joining the group. My affection for the Grand Canyon mirrored Brer Rabbit's for the briar patch. There were no other places I would rather hike. Without hesitation I told John to count me in. I had planned such a trek in October 1996 but managed to complete only one crossing (R2R), as my hiking companions and I had neither strength nor energy for a round trip. Could a fifty-eight-year-old accomplish what he failed to complete ten years earlier?

We planned to start our trip after the North Rim officially opened in mid-May and needed to complete it before early June, when one of our group, Benjamin "Benji" Williams, reported to Naval Officer Indoctrination School in Newport, Rhode Island. Calendars were checked, dates were selected—Memorial Day weekend—six months in the future, but none too early to make lodging reservations on the North and South Rims and to start physically preparing for the rigorous trip.

Joining John, Benji, and me were John's friend, Chris Beck, and Chris' father Rick, an ophthalmologist in Newton, Kansas. I implored everyone to do whatever it took to get in shape, although I contend the best way to prepare for a hike in the Grand Canyon is to hike in the Grand Canyon. Hiking in the Canyon involved long sections of downhill walking and equally long sections of uphill walking, often on a brutally hot day. Kansas could be brutally hot, but usually not until June—after we returned from the hike—and Kansas could offer no topography like the Grand Canyon. Nevertheless, training in Kansas would have to suffice. In January 2006 I started a program of jogging and walking in preparation for the long hike. Two weeks before departure I walked eleven miles on the flatlands of central Kansas in three and a half hours and still had life in my legs; however, this was not equivalent to walking across the Grand Canyon twice in three days.

The month before our hike, Chris Beck fell ill with strep throat and infectious mononucleosis and subsequently developed pneumonia. By mid-May his condition had improved but he had not fully recovered. He had neither strength nor stamina for a trans-canyon walk. Rick thought he and Chris should abandon the trip, although they finally decided to travel to the Grand Canyon but not hike. One week before leaving for Arizona I developed acute prostatitis, which slowed me down but did not deter me from a Grand Canyon hike. It would take more than this infection to keep me away from the Canyon.

Wanting an early start in order to complete the major portion of the crossing in the cooler morning hours, John, Benji, and I awakened at 3:00 AM on Friday morning, May 26. Rick transported us the two miles from our cabin to the North Kaibab trailhead. At 3:28 AM, we said our good-byes to Rick, promising to meet him and Chris on the South Rim later that day. Rick and Chris would drive the two hundred fifteen miles—ten times the distance we would walk—to the South Rim. Shivering from the cold pre-dawn temperature and the excitement of the adventure, I led the way down the steep, dusty path. The rhythmic tapping of trekking poles against rock complemented the early morning calls of birds and the rustle of wind in the trees. A strong wind kicked up trail dust that, when illuminated by our headlamps, had the appearance of a fine mist.

The steep descent did not immediately bother my knees. Often after a few miles of downhill walking I developed pain in the outside of one or both knees. I hoped this malady would not plague me this trip. We reached the Supai Tunnel (two-mile mark) in fifty-four minutes and shortly thereafter it became light enough to turn off our headlamps. The night chill disappeared as quickly as drops of water on a hot griddle. We changed into shorts and short-sleeved shirts. By the two hour forty-four minute mark we reached the pumping station caretaker's house below Roaring Springs and refilled our hydration system reservoirs. Each of us carried small packs carrying hydration systems, permitting us to sip water whenever we desired during the hike. We also carried high energy, lightweight foods for the long walk.

After Roaring Springs the trail leveled and our pace quickened. We passed or were passed by numerous hikers sharing our goal of crossing the Canyon in one day. John, Benji, and I were not the only visitors ignoring the park rangers' warnings against such a strenuous day outing. In fact, there appeared to be more people on the trail intent on crossing the Canyon in one day than those taking the recommended two to three days. My calculation was based on direct questioning, as well as observation. When I saw athletic-looking young adults in running garb, carrying only small daypacks or fanny packs and hydration systems, I suspected they were attempting what we were attempting. Individuals carrying large packs were arbitrarily omitted from the crossing-the-canyon-in-a-day group.

The thermometer on a bulletin board at Cottonwood Campground registered seventy-two degrees—quite a change from the near-freezing temperature on the North Rim three hours earlier. During the ensuing gentle downhill seven-mile walk from Cottonwood to the Colorado River I listened to music on my iPod, first *The Soundtrack from Everest,* followed by Pink Floyd's *The Wall.* Listening to recorded music in the Grand Canyon could be considered sacrilegious when the Canyon offered the calls of insects and birds, the rustling of leaves in the wind, and the gurgle of water rushing over rocks. Nevertheless, I succumbed to temptation as I rambled along the stream. The music interfered with hearing the chatter of Benji and John walking behind me, but the noisy flow of Bright Angel Creek and the distinctive call of canyon wrens could still be heard.

We reached Bright Angel Campground at 9:52 AM—completing fourteen miles in less than six hours—well ahead of my pace crossing the Canyon in 1996. A thermometer in the shade read eighty-six degrees upon our arrival at the campground; an inner canyon high of near one hundred degrees was predicted. Water containers were refilled, calories were consumed, and legs were rested before trudging on—up the Bright Angel Trail rather than the shorter, steeper, and more sun-exposed South Kaibab Trail. I was concerned that we could not carry enough water for a climb up the South Kaibab Trail on a hot afternoon, and there were no water sources between the river and the rim on that route. In contrast, drinking water sources existed at four and a half, six, and seven and a half miles up the Bright Angel Trail.

Upon leaving Bright Angel Campground I soaked my shirt and the bandana around my neck in the cold water of Bright Angel Creek. Within minutes they were dry. Crossing the Colorado River on the Silver Bridge I became acutely aware of the heat and my energy evaporated as quickly as the water on my shirt. I was glad to be hiking out of the inner canyon before it became even hotter. I would follow the advice I had preached to novice hikers in the Grand Canyon—avoid hiking when it is extraordinarily hot, drink plenty of water, and take it easy, or become the latest in a long list of victims of the harsh Canyon environment catalogued by Ghiglieri and Myers in their book, *Over the Edge: Death in Grand Canyon*.

John, Benji, and I slogged through the sand dunes along the south bank of the river to the foot of Bright Angel Trail at Pipe Creek and started the climb to Indian Garden. It took us two hours and forty minutes to walk from Bright Angel Campground to Indian Garden—my goal of averaging two miles per hour for the crossing in jeopardy. Was maintaining a two miles per hour pace really that important?

On the infrequent, short downhill stretches of the trail I experienced pain at the outside of my right knee. Despite my pre-hike conditioning program and use of trekking poles I had not avoided this affliction after all. I yelped but plodded on, thankful, paradoxically, that it was uphill the rest of the way.

After spending thirty-five minutes at Indian Garden, rehydrating and consuming a few more calories, we began the push to the top. The trail was in terrible shape—deeply rutted from mule traffic. Deep depressions in the path could not be stepped over or around. Going uphill was hard enough, stepping in and out of potholes in the earth made travel even worse. I found it impossible to develop a rhythm in my stride and silently cursed the mules, even though they were an integral element of Grand Canyon lore, carrying tourists and cargo up and down Bright Angel and South Kaibab Trails, pulverizing the earthen trail bed with their hooves, and causing the deep ruts. As an added bonus they also left their droppings and urine for two-legged beasts to endure.

My pace gradually slowed as I trudged up the Jacob's Ladder switchbacks in The Redwall. The warm afternoon, the uphill grade, the obstacle course of a trail, and twenty miles of walking had extracted its toll. I wondered if it would have been easier climbing out on the steeper but shorter South Kaibab Trail. The Three-Mile Resthouse provided a welcome respite from my labors—a shady place to rest, rehydrate, and consume a few more calories. My next goal was the One-and-a-Half-Mile Resthouse—halfway to the rim from the Three-Mile Resthouse. An hour later I passed the One-and-a-Half-Mile Resthouse but stubbornly refused to stop until I reached the rim. The warm water remaining in my hydration system would see me through. The boys let me proceed alone while they halted for fresh, cool water. In a matter of minutes they caught up with me and stayed on my heels until we finally emerged from the Canyon at 5:04 PM—thirteen hours, thirty-six minutes, and thirteen seconds after our early morning start—five minutes slower than my crossing in 1996. I felt better after this crossing than the crossing in 1996 but my low back and right knee hurt and my energy level registered zero. A return walk to the North Rim seemed doubtful.

We were wise to take a day off between Canyon crossings. Ibuprofen and a day of rest did wonders for my aching muscles and joints. By Saturday night I felt better and decided to walk back to the North Rim with Benji and John. The boys were willing to slow their pace for me, and Benji agreed to carry some of my food and water to lighten my already light load.

Rick deposited us at the South Kaibab Trailhead near Yaki Point at 4:50 AM on Sunday morning—twenty-five minutes before official sunrise, but light enough to see the trail without headlamps. Like the Bright Angel Trail, the South Kaibab Trail was deeply rutted by mule-train traffic. We stepped in and out of deep depressions in the earth between timber crossbeams placed at intervals to retard erosion. The steep downhill grade aggravated the pain on the outside of my right knee caused by repetitive rubbing of a tendon (the iliotibial band) across the bony protuberance on the outside of my knee (lateral epicondyle of the femur). I used my trekking poles as crutches to keep from bending my knee. Passing walkers must have wondered what a gimpy old man was doing hiking across the Canyon. We reached the Colorado River in a painfully slow three hours and fifty-three minutes, crossed the Kaibab Suspension Bridge and proceeded to Phantom Ranch. I looked forward to easier walking on the gentle incline through Bright Angel Canyon.

I do not believe I have ever been at Phantom Ranch in more glorious weather. The temperature was in the eighties with a high of ninety predicted, rather than the usual one hundred degrees. A strong breeze rustled the leaves on the cottonwoods. The speckled pattern of shadows cast by the leaves gave Phantom Ranch the appearance of a pointillist painting. We sat in the shade on a bench outside the dining hall, consuming fluids, energy bars, and nuts, and observed the comings and goings of guests at Phantom Ranch. After a thirty minute break we were off, walking in the morning shade in The Box for the next three miles. My knee did not hurt walking on level ground and our pace exceeded two miles per hour. Full sunlight greeted us once we emerged from The Box, but the temperature stayed in the eighties. It took approximately three hours to complete the seven miles from Phantom Ranch to Cottonwood—only seven miles to go to the top. I did not relish the remaining uphill haul but moderate temperatures and a refreshing breeze made the climb less daunting.

Near the turnoff to the day use area at Roaring Springs I encountered a gentleman who appeared to be in his late sixties or early seventies heading downhill with a full pack. He took one look at my shuffling gait, the grimace on my face, the sweat on my brow, and the small pack on my back and correctly deduced that I was crossing the Canyon in one day. He expressed more disdain than regard for my endeavor and actually told me to "slow down and smell the flowers." I could not go much slower, and I was too tired to stick my nose in a cactus bloom.

A short time later we stopped to talk with a park ranger walking down the trail. She asked us how we were doing and how far we had traveled that day. Upon learning of our transcanyon walk she responded, "You don't look too bad, keep it up." I had no choice. Buoyed by the ranger's words of encouragement, I walked on—stopping sparingly and briefly. As hard as it was to put one foot in front of the other, it was even harder to resume walking after stopping. John and Benji followed me, probably wondering if the old man would make it, but never criticized my pace. The Canyon colors were vivid—blue sky, red canyon walls, green foliage on trees and bushes, yellow blooms on prickly pear cacti—the beauty of the place appreciated despite the discomfort of the moment.

While Benji, John, and I walked across the Grand Canyon, Rick and Chris drove back to the North Rim. Upon arriving at the North Rim, Chris meandered down the North Kaibab Trail, meeting us just above the bridge in the Redwall layer in Roaring Springs Canyon.

Shadows lengthened as we hiked through the top layers of the Canyon. The boys chatted incessantly as they leisurely followed me up the trail. I frequently sipped water and periodically consumed a package of high-energy gel. I recited the mantra—"Know the Canyon's History, Study Rocks Made By Time"—used to remember the nine rock layers in the Canyon from rim to the top of the Grand Canyon Supergroup

(Kaibab Limestone, Toroweap Formation, Coconino Sandstone, Hermit Shale, Supai Formation, Redwall Limestone, Muav Limestone, Bright Angel Shale, and Tapeats Sandstone). It sure seemed like the trail was in "study" a long time.

After passing through the Supai Tunnel I was ready for a musical interlude and fished my iPod out of my daypack. It was now time to hike in the Grand Canyon listening to Ferde Grofe's *Grand Canyon Suite*—the reason for bringing my iPod in the first place. Inspired by a trip to the Grand Canyon in 1916, Grofe composed the first movement, "Sunrise," in 1929, and completed an additional four movements, "Painted Desert," "On the Trail," "Sunset," and "Cloudburst," in 1931. The pace of the mule train Grofe musically portrayed in "On the Trail" proved too fast for me but the music momentarily diverted my attention from the struggle of the uphill climb.

Finally, the trail leveled and I saw blue sky rather than canyon wall ahead. Rick Beck stood at the trailhead. In an act of bravado I trotted the last few yards up the trail—the double traverse successfully completed at 5:51 PM—walking from South Rim to North Rim in thirteen hours and one minute. Although the North Kaibab Trailhead was 1,400 vertical feet higher than the Bright Angel Trailhead on the South Rim, I felt stronger climbing out the north side than the south two days earlier—presumably because of the cooler weather, shaded trail, and three less miles of walking.

John, Benji, and I were beat—forty-four horizontal miles and 21,000 feet of ascent and descent in three days—not exactly equivalent to climbing Mt. Everest, although climbing from Everest base camp (17,600 feet) to summit (29,028 feet) and back is a total ascent and descent of 22,856 feet. Due to a poor choice of footwear (we wore mountain running shoes rather than hiking boots), the long walk, or a combination of both, each of us developed blisters on both feet. They were the first blisters I had suffered since hiking in the Grand Canyon in 1974. The blisters would heal. The beauty of the Grand Canyon, the elation of successfully completing a physical challenge, and the bliss felt each time I dropped below the rim on a hike would not be forgotten. But it was more than the hike that attracted me to the Canyon. A hike could be taken in many places closer to home. The Grand Canyon was a sacred place. A walk in the Canyon recharged my spiritual battery as much as it depleted my physical battery. My appreciation of the beauty of nature, the connection between man and nature, and of the divine strengthened.

Apparently John Muir did not approve of the word "hike." In *The Mountain Trail and Its Message,* published in 1911, Albert W. Palmer tells the story of meeting John Muir on the trail and asking him if he indeed disliked the word "hike." Muir replied:

> I don't like either the word or the thing. People ought to saunter in the mountains—not hike! ... Do you know the origin of the word "saunter?" It's a beautiful word. Away back in the Middle Ages people used to go on pilgrimages to the Holy Land, and when people in the villages through which they passed asked where they were going, they would reply, "A la sainte tere," "To the Holy Land." And so they became known as sainte-terre-ers or saunterers. Now these mountains are our Holy Land, and we ought to saunter through them reverently, not "hike" through them.

The Grand Canyon is definitely a holy land for me. I will try to saunter through it in the future.

Chapter 16
Old Trail, New Experience

May 2007

Hearing that we were hiking across the Canyon the next day, our waiter at Grand Canyon Lodge on the North Rim asked if we had heard about the exploits of Maverick. The only "Maverick" I knew was the television show aired in the nineteen sixties.

"No, I haven't heard about Maverick," I replied.

"Well," he interjected, "upon turning eighty, Maverick decided to hike across the Grand Canyon eighty times before his eighty-first birthday. He eventually crossed the Canyon one hundred and four times in one year."

"Have you met Maverick?" I inquired.

"No," he replied," but I think I passed him on the trail once."

I wondered if Maverick really existed. Amazing—a hundred and four Canyon crossings in one year by an octogenarian. Until hearing about the adventures of Maverick, I felt pretty smug about crossing the Canyon eight times in forty-five years. My achievements were trivial compared to Maverick's. Perhaps the feats of Maverick were exaggerated, but I couldn't get it out of my mind—a hundred and four crossings in one year, by an old geezer to boot.

Only a hike—or saunter—in the Grand Canyon could make me eagerly jump out of bed at 2:00 AM. Like a kid unable to sleep Christmas Eve night in anticipation of the treasures he might find under the tree

Christmas morning, I slept fitfully and would have started an hour earlier if my companions had consented.

My son John, his imperturbable roommate and Portland musician and songwriter, Chris Beck, now fully recovered from the illness that sidelined him the previous year, and my friend and frequent hiking companion, John Divine, were rousted out of bed. The boys groused about the early morning wake-up call but dutifully prepared to leave for the trailhead. On the other hand, Divine shared my excitement to commence the stroll I had proposed to him several months earlier—walking across the Canyon in one day, resting a day, and returning on foot the following day. The aches and pains of my last Canyon trip long forgotten, I wanted to repeat the trek made with my son and Benji Williams in May 2006.

Within two weeks of making the decision to hike in Grand Canyon, my son and Chris Beck, recent émigrés to Portland, Oregon, were invited to join Divine and me. Both boys promised to stay fit by walking, running, and biking in Portland. I had little doubt that they would be in great physical shape for the hike, as long as they avoided illness. Divine and I hoped we could keep up with them.

John Divine had hiked in the Canyon on six previous occasions and had completed seven marathons. He reassured me that, despite being five years my senior and not as trim as he once was, he was capable of completing the walk—a forty-one mile round trip with 21,000 vertical feet of ascent and descent—if he did some serious training. Divine and I walked many miles in and around Salina preparing for the rugged trek. Realizing that there were few level paths in Grand Canyon, we repeatedly walked up and down the lone hill in Salina and another taller hill in the country south of town. I cranked up the treadmill at the local YMCA to its maximum fifteen percent grade and set the speed to two miles per hour in an attempt to simulate the incline I would encounter and the pace I wanted to maintain climbing out of the Canyon.

At 2:55 AM we started down the North Kaibab Trail, an early start necessary to complete the fourteen miles to the Colorado River and climb out of the Inner Gorge to the Tonto Plateau before it became brutally hot. In late May daytime high temperatures in the bottom of the Canyon can soar above one hundred degrees, and walking during the hot hours of the day rated at the bottom of my list of favorite things to do. If we started our saunter across the Canyon later in the morning, I was afraid we would have to bivouac in the shade in the inner canyon during mid-day and delay our exit to the South Rim until late afternoon, when it would be cooler.

The thermometer dangling from my pack read fifty-five degrees as we started down the trail. The sky was clear and it was deathly quiet—no wind rustling the trees, no insect noises, and no birdcalls. Only the thud of boots hitting the earth and the clicking of trekking pole tips hitting rock disturbed the silence. Each of us wore headlamps to illuminate the trail. As on the trip a year earlier, a fine dust suspended in the air clouded our vision. Although not physically exhausting, walking downhill in the dark dictated a slow pace and required constant vigilance as to where we placed our feet—a mentally exhausting chore. Fortunately, no one tumbled in the dark. Had we started down after daybreak, I believe we could have completed the descent much faster, but the faster pace would have been more tiring and sapped strength needed for the climb to the South Rim later in the day.

We reached the two-mile mark at Supai Tunnel at the top of the Supai Formation within forty-eight minutes. Insects now serenaded us, and clear skies had given way to a blanket of clouds that intermittently unleashed a few raindrops.

After nearly two hours of walking in the dark we turned off our headlamps, and the Canyon became more than a dark wall to our right, emptiness to the left, and a few feet of trail seen in the beam of our flashlights. Daylight revealed the magnificent dimensions and glorious colors of a truly grand canyon. Birds called out their welcome—mimicking John Divine's trademark greeting, "Have a great day."

At 5:45 AM we reached the Roaring Springs pump house caretaker's front yard. For as long as I can remember the caretaker displayed a sign welcoming hikers to rest a spell in his yard and refill their canteens at his faucet. From 1973 until 2006 Bruce Aiken and his wife Mary tended the water supply at Roaring Springs. They raised three children in their canyon home. Often the children would offer lemonade to passing hikers. A trained artist, Aiken captured the beauty and many moods of the Grand Canyon in his paintings. His art is the subject of Susan McGarry's book, *Bruce Aiken's Grand Canyon, An Intimate Affair*. After leaving the Canyon Mr. Aiken moved to Flagstaff, Arizona, where he has a studio. In the past year a new manager had taken up residence in Roaring Springs.

On the trail near the caretaker's house I nearly stepped on a giant hairy scorpion (*Hadrurus spadix*) the size of my index finger. This nonlethal species dwarfed any I had previously seen in the Canyon. A nocturnal hunter, the scorpion was late returning to its daytime hideout. It graciously posed for photographs for several minutes before sauntering into the rocks at the side of the trail. Six species of scorpion reside in the Canyon and only the slender scorpion or Arizona bark scorpion (*Centruroides sculptuatus*) is potentially lethal to humans. Allegedly its venom is more potent than that of a rattlesnake.

John Divine, John Cathcart-Rake, and Chris Beck on bridge over Bright Angel Creek

Another half hour of walking brought us to Cottonwood Campground—the first third of our traverse completed—nearly seven miles in three and a half hours. My son had brought a powdered product that when mixed in water and consumed promised to provide essential nutrients for the vigorous task of the day. This sports drink had the appearance of stagnant pond water and tasted even worse. How could something touted to be so good for you be so vile? Chris and John considered it medicine—preferring to chug it by the liter at rest stops rather than sip it as they walked. I swore I would vomit if I chugged it and dumped the cloudy liquid on the surrounding shrubs and refilled my container with tap water, later joking that the boy's sports drink probably killed those plants.

The middle third of the hike was the easiest leg, a 7.2-mile jaunt down a trail following Bright Angel Creek from Cottonwood to Phantom Ranch. Only a short climb up Asinine Hill near the turnoff to Ribbon Falls interrupted an otherwise gentle downhill grade.

The sky remained overcast, and the air temperature remained mercifully cool. A pair of cross-canyon runners passed us on their way north. I suspected that once they reached the North Rim they would turn around and head back to the South Rim, completing a rim-to-rim-to-rim run later that evening. Ultrarunners were attracted to the forty-one mile run despite the park service's warning against such long excursions in short periods of time.

Prickly pear cacti *Opuntia* or paddle cactus), bearing red or yellow blooms, and century plants (*Agave utabensis*) decorated our route. The prickly pear cactus is armed with two kinds of spines—an ominous-looking, large, smooth, fixed spine and a small hairlike spine capable of easily penetrating the skin and detaching from the plant. This tiny spine is difficult to remove once embedded in the skin and can produce severe pain. Because of its ability to store water the prickly pear cactus can survive years without rainfall.

Century plants are found throughout the canyon from elevations of 1,200 feet to 7,000 feet. It was originally thought that the agave bloomed only once a century, thus the name century plant. Actually, fifteen to twenty-five years after emerging, the century plant sends out a single tall, flowering stalk, drops its seed, and dies.

We arrived at Phantom Ranch six and a half hours after starting the hike—plopping down for a rest at the picnic tables outside the dining hall. My son complained of feeling groggy for the first fourteen miles of the hike, never totally conscious after his 2:00 AM wake-up call until reaching Phantom Ranch. I mistakenly attributed his near silence to his laconic character rather than sleepwalking.

During the break I met a deeply tanned, wiry old man, missing a front tooth and wearing a black stocking cap emblazoned with a University of Colorado logo. A fellow CU alumnus, I thought. It turned out he once attended classes at the CU campus in Denver. In more ways than one he appeared to have a lot of miles on him. After exchanging greetings the topic quickly turned to hiking in the Grand Canyon. He claimed that he had been camping in the Grand Canyon for the past seven days and planned on exiting the canyon in two days via the North Kaibab Trail. Shortly thereafter he planned a hike to Nankoweap Creek in the eastern Grand Canyon—allegedly the most difficult hike on a named trail in the Canyon. This guy impressed me as a veteran Grand Canyon hiker. I then inquired, "Have you met Maverick?"

"Yes, had lunch with him on Thanksgiving Day while hiking in the Canyon," he replied. "He invited me to visit him at his home on the South Rim, but I never made it."

"Did he really hike across the Canyon a hundred and four times in the year after turning eighty?" I queried.

He didn't know, but went on to share an observation: "Something happens when you turn eighty—your intellectual powers may start to fail but a new drive to undertake incomprehensible physical tasks emerges." I presumed this was his explanation for Maverick's quest and wondered if my insatiable appetite for hiking in the Grand Canyon meant I was losing my mind at the young age of fifty-eight.

I would have plenty of time to contemplate the old-timer's wisdom on the hike out. Shouldering daypacks containing extra shoes, a change of clothes, water, food, and toiletries, we headed for the start of the South Kaibab Trail at the south end of Kaibab Suspension Bridge spanning the Colorado River. Within minutes of starting the climb it became obvious why the South Kaibab Trail was not a favored exit route to the South Rim. It was a steep, sun-exposed trail with no sources of drinking water. On a hot day it can be a brutal climb. With the weather cool and cloudy it remained a tough climb.

South Kaibab Trail, Tonto Plateau

The grade and uneven footing of South Kaibab Trail exceeded anything I encountered on the hills of central Kansas and the treadmill at the gym, but I felt strong climbing the switchbacks through the Vishnu Complex, Grand Canyon Supergroup, and Tapeats Sandstone. The trail was in excellent condition—absent were the huge divots dug into the path by mule traffic; a maintenance crew had repaired the trail since my previous trip. "This isn't so bad," I told Divine. However, upon reaching The Tipoff on the Tonto Plateau and realizing that four and a half miles of difficult walking lay ahead, my outlook changed. Fatigue gently tapped me on the shoulder, and then grabbed me with a tight fist. It had Divine in a bear hold. Any idea of a quick exit from the Canyon evaporated.

As we climbed through the Muav Limestone it started raining. I rummaged through my pack for my rain jacket and once it was retrieved, the squall passed. Back into the pack went the jacket.

A half mile below Cedar Ridge, John Divine and I met a National Park Ranger headed towards Phantom Ranch. He had been working at Grand Canyon for thirteen years—hiking an estimated 8,000 miles below the rim in that span. He couldn't imagine working anywhere else. Hiking in Grand Canyon can become an obsession—how better to explain this ranger's mileage, Maverick's alleged feats, and my nearly fifty years of hiking in the Canyon?

Upon reaching Cedar Ridge, a mile and a half below the rim, John Divine complained of leg cramps and insisted that the boys and I not slow down for him. He assured me he would not be far behind. Chris, John, and I plodded on, but Chris and John soon decided to quicken the pace and left me behind. Slowly but surely, huffing and puffing, I climbed through the Coconino, Toroweap, and Kaibab layers to the top—finishing the crossing shortly after 3:00 PM—twelve hours, seventeen minutes, and fifty seconds after starting—my fastest Canyon crossing.

Looking back down the trail Divine was nowhere in sight. Approximately ten minutes after I reached the top, a group of young men reached the trailhead and one of them asked me if I was in the group from Kansas that had just completed a north to south crossing.

"Yes," I replied.

They had passed John Divine at least fifteen minutes earlier and, concerned about his miserable appearance, given him an energy bar to eat. They thought a few calories might avert collapse.

"He looks bad," one hiker claimed.

"I'm not sure he can make it out," another added.

Expecting to find Divine lying on the trail, Chris and I hustled back down the path we had ascended. We reached John taking baby steps on the trail—ready to attack the series of switchbacks known as The Chimney cut into the Kaibab Limestone, the last rock layer before the rim. He looked spent, but was still capable of walking. I took his pack and encouraged him onward, affirming that the end was in sight. He wondered what "the end" meant. I asserted that he could still complete the crossing in less than thirteen hours if he kept moving. Like a horse given the whip, he bolted forward—topping out with fifteen seconds to spare. He had made it, but could he walk back to the North Rim after a day of rest? The broad smile that typically graced Divine's face had been replaced with a look of total exhaustion.

A good meal at El Tovar and a soft bed in a motel room at Yavapai Lodge were our rewards for completing a long walk. Thunderstorms moved through the area during the night, dumping much-needed rain on the parched Grand Canyon. I periodically awakened to flashes of lightning, the boom of thunder, and rain lashing against the window, happy to be in a motel room rather than in a tent, and even happier that I was not starting a hike across the Canyon in this weather.

Clouds blanketed the giant chasm that morning like a plug of cotton hiding the contents of a newly opened pill bottle. A century earlier, John Hance, allegedly the first non-native resident at Grand Canyon, tried to convince visitors that he attempted to cross a similarly cloud-packed canyon on snowshoes, only to be stranded on a solitary peak when the clouds dissipated. Walking from rim to rim on the clouds sure would have been a shorter and more level path than the one walked the previous day. While I pondered a route to the North Rim, the clouds evaporated—a theater curtain rising to reveal a master set designer's creation.

From Kolb Studio on the South Rim we saw an elegantly grotesque California condor with its nine-foot wingspan soaring on an updraft in the Canyon. The condor flew within forty feet of our observation point at the studio. In the 1980s the California condor, after living in the area for 50,000 years, nearly joined a growing list of extinct animals. An estimated twenty-two California condors existed. After a program of captive breeding the California condor was reintroduced to the wild, first in California in 1992, then at the Vermillion Cliffs in northern Arizona in 1995, and more recently at Grand Canyon. In the spring of

2004 the first condor to fledge in the wild since 1982, joined his fellow condors in the skies above the Grand Canyon.

Despite the hardship of the first crossing, I gave no thought to returning to the North Rim by means other than my own legs. John Divine knew he could return to the North Rim on the shuttle but reassured me that he had recovered enough to join the boys and me for the return hike. Chris and my son valued sleep more than an early start to a return walk to the North Rim. They requested not to be awakened at whatever ungodly hour Divine and I intended to arise. Powered by their noxious sports drink, they would catch up with us in the Canyon later.

My watch alarm beeped at 3:30 AM on Thursday. I could have used a few more hours of sleep but knew we would not reach the North Rim before dark if we did not get an early start from the South Rim. A late arrival on the North Rim also meant missing our dinner reservations at the lodge. John and I would rather get up early than miss a great meal. I called a cab to transport us several miles east to the South Kaibab trailhead.

Chris and my son remained asleep in an adjacent motel room. Later they found a note slipped under their door, informing them of our departure. At 4:10 AM Divine and I started down the South Kaibab Trail, needing headlamps for the first forty minutes of our descent. We had the Canyon to ourselves—no other headlamps bobbed up and down in the dark. Over the eastern canyon I witnessed the prelude to sunrise—the horizon ablaze like a Kansas prairie fire at night—another special moment in the Grand Canyon comparable to witnessing the sunset at Plateau Point or on the Esplanade, sitting by the edge of Bright Angel Creek at nightfall with good friends, and looking up and down Middle Granite Gorge from above on my Thunder River hike.

Puddles from the drenching showers of twenty-four hours earlier dotted the trail. We were blessed with another great day for a hike—cool, clear, and trail dust settled by the recent rain. At a rest stop on the Tonto Platform John Divine read aloud from the book he had carried with him, the *Tao Te Ching* of Lao-tzu. The author expounded on the sacredness of the world and warned that tampering with the earth would only ruin it. John claimed it was a randomly selected reading. I could not have selected a more appropriate reading for the day.

John Divine and I arrived at Phantom Ranch at 8:00 AM—by my standards, a relatively slow descent from rim to river, but by John Divine's standards, an ideal pace. Chris and my son had not intercepted us. Were they out of bed yet? After a short break Divine and I left Phantom Ranch for the walk along Bright Angel Creek to Cottonwood Campground. I scrawled short messages in several different muddy spots on the trail above Phantom Ranch: our initials, "J & B," and the time we reached this point. I hoped that at least one of the notes would survive the foot traffic on the trail and would be correctly interpreted by the boys.

Divine and I circumvented the climb up Asinine Hill at the Ribbon Falls turnoff, choosing to cross Bright Angel Creek on stepping stones, bushwhack along the western bank of the stream and then cross the creek on a footbridge before continuing on the trail to Cottonwood. Although a diversion from the usual route, this detour saved little, if any, time or energy. Perhaps Asinine Hill was not so asinine after all.

Chris and John had not caught up with us when we reached Cottonwood at noon. I knew they could take care of themselves but wondered where they were. A mile beyond Cottonwood we crossed Bright Angel Creek and stopped at the Roaring Springs pump house caretaker's yard for a breather and to replenish our water stores for the 3.8-mile climb to the Supai Tunnel, our next source of water. A small group of through-hikers passed us at Roaring Springs and informed us that they had met Chris and John at Cottonwood—the first official confirmation that they were on the trail and on our tail.

I could not believe our luck. Despite sunny skies the afternoon temperature remained in the seventies—unusually cool for this time of day and season. A strong breeze evaporated the sweat soaking my shirt, contributing to my comfort.

At the bottom of the Redwall the boys finally caught up with John Divine and me. They had started down the South Kaibab Trail at 6:15 AM in hot pursuit of the old men and would have reached us earlier had they not taken a side trip to Ribbon Falls, where they showered and ate lunch. Chris and John did see my messages etched into the trail between Phantom Ranch and the Ribbon Falls turnoff and correctly deciphered their meaning. They reported that other hikers had mistaken my cryptic notes scrawled in the earth as Bible verses.

Divine and I were not capable of maintaining the boys' pace for another three and a half miles to the top. We waved them on, giving them the keys to the car and my credit card as they passed, requesting that they drive the two miles from the trailhead to Grand Canyon Lodge and register and get the keys to our cabin. "Don't forget to return for us," I added.

Plodding on, we climbed the multiple switchbacks through the Supai Formation, stopping at the rest area just above the Supai Tunnel for fresh water. I consumed a bottle of sports drink of my choice (in contrast to the swill the boys drank) and delighted in the sweetness of a candy bar that had survived the walk across the Canyon.

Between Supai Tunnel and the rim the trail became congested with hikers—some taking a short, late afternoon stroll down the trail and others, like us, climbing out of the Canyon after spending many hours below the rim. The earth turned from red in the Supai Formation and Hermit Shale to brown in the higher layers—color changes we did not appreciate descending in the dark sixty hours earlier.

The sugar fix at the Supai Tunnel must have helped—my legs held out for the final two miles. Before I knew it the trail leveled out in the Kaibab Limestone and the noise of cars whizzing by the trailhead could be heard. I exited the Canyon at 4:32 PM—twelve hours and twenty-two minutes after starting the crossing in the dark earlier that day. John Divine arrived at the trailhead seven minutes later. He looked much better than he did climbing out the South Rim—a smile, rather than a dazed look, graced his face. My son and Chris, who had hiked out in nine hours fifteen minutes and nine hours and twenty minutes, respectively, returned with the car and ferried us to our cabin.

No sightings or word of Maverick on our south to north crossing. Later I learned that Maverick existed. His real name was Laurent Gaudreau, and he celebrated his eightieth birthday in 2006. Maverick had an obsession for hiking the corridor trails of the Grand Canyon and crossed the Canyon over a hundred times during his eightieth year. I could not imagine walking across the Grand Canyon a hundred times in a year and remained satisfied with my ten crossings in forty-six years and four crossings in the past three hundred sixty-three days. This trip was particularly satisfying because I had minimal pain and stiffness during and after the hike, and absolutely no knee pain. Perhaps my training program in Kansas during the months prior to the hike paid off.

Although I have crossed the Grand Canyon multiple times since 1961, this trip was remarkable for the ease in which I identified each rock layer. More attentive to the flora and fauna of the Canyon, I added to the list of plants and animals I could identify. A quick crossing of Grand Canyon was not incompatible with learning something new and enjoying the view. Without the burden of a heavy pack it was easier to take breaks to investigate interesting sights along the trail and to take photographs.

Despite hiking the same trail time and again, I never grow tired of the Canyon. The spiritual awakening afforded by a walk below the rim, a bonding experience with friends, the unparalleled beauty of the place, a chance to study the geology, flora, and fauna of the Canyon, and an escape from the noise and corruption of life in civilization all called me back. There was always something new to discover—seeing something familiar in a different light or noticing a geologic formation or rock or plant for the first time even though I had passed by it multiple times. The camaraderie on the trail and the endorphin high of the physical challenge added to the pleasure. My story is not unique. This trip I met a park ranger that had hiked 8,000 miles during a thirteen-year stint in the Canyon and heard of Maverick's quest. Hundreds of individuals return innumerable times to hike in the Grand Canyon—walking more miles and to more destinations than I can fathom. Undoubtedly each person has his or her own reason for returning to hike in Grand Canyon, but one thing is certain, Grand Canyon grabs you—and will not let you go.

Chapter 17
Another Amazing Day

September 2008

What could I possibly say about a journey in the Grand Canyon I had made ten times before? Of course, there had been changes since I first walked across the Grand Canyon on the main corridor trails in 1961. The transformations had been relatively minor; for example, since completion of Glen Canyon Dam in 1963 the Colorado River often ran green rather than brown and since the mid-1960s the Silver Bridge spanned the river a short distance downstream from the Kaibab Bridge. Improvements had been made in the North Kaibab Trail and new bridges spanned Bright Angel Creek. Perhaps the biggest change in the past half-century had been the marked increase in the number of visitors to the Canyon. Nevertheless, the geologic profile of the place had not changed. In the nearly fifty years I had been visiting the Grand Canyon the river had deepened it little more than the width of a pencil lead.

In contrast to the Grand Canyon my physical characteristics had changed considerably since I had first crossed the Canyon as a skinny twelve-year-old kid. I had grown taller and gained weight. My feet had become flat and my hair had turned white. My strength and endurance peaked in my thirties and forties and was now ebbing, and my walking speed had slowed considerably. My pace in 2008 was probably not much faster than the pace I maintained in 1961 as an initiate to Grand

Canyon hiking. However, my enthusiasm for hiking in the Canyon had not diminished.

At the time of my first hike in the Canyon I had no idea what career pathway I wanted to take. Since then I completed high school, college, medical school, and postgraduate training and established a practice in Salina, Kansas. Over the years I transitioned myself from a general internist to a specialist in cancer medicine (medical oncology) with the attendant stresses of caring for a very special population of patients requiring a great deal of my time and energy. Trekking in Grand Canyon provided temporary respite from the demands of my profession. Some would call it recreation. I would call it "re-creation."

The question lingered. What new and significant facet of knowledge might be revealed on my eleventh crossing of the Canyon and sixth crossing in one day on the main corridor trails? Contemplating a response to the question, I recalled the first line of an e. e. cummings poem I read in a college English class in the 1960s: "i thank You God for most this amazing day." The answer was obvious: I was given a new day to celebrate life and the beauty of creation around me. What could be more significant? Let the day unfold and enjoy it rather than consciously search for some weighty experience. I entered the Canyon again.

In late winter 2007 fellow Salinan Charley Griffin asked me when it would be his turn to walk with me in the Canyon. "When do you want to go?" I replied. We set a date in late September 2008. Deciding against camping in the Canyon, we chose to walk across the gorge in one day (rim-to-rim)—not a novel endeavor for me but a great way to see a lot of the Grand Canyon in a relatively short period of time. In addition, since we were not going to stay overnight in the Canyon the cumbersome process of obtaining a camping permit could be avoided.

Two other friends, John Divine and Jack Ropp, also wanted to accompany us to the Canyon but did not want to participate in the walk. John had joined me on the hike in May 2007 and no longer trusted his legs on such a long day hike. Jack had no interest in any long walk, no matter the locale, but was interested in a road trip with the guys. Jack and John volunteered to travel with Charley and me to the South Kaibab trailhead near Grand Canyon Village on the South Rim. After seeing us off, they would drive the two hundred fifteen miles to the North Rim and meet us at the North Kaibab trailhead.

Several weeks before our departure for the Canyon another Salina friend, Jim Manley, asked if he could join Charley and me on our rim-to-rim hike. Jim, also known as The Animal because of his strenuous conditioning program, was traveling to the Southwest with his wife and anticipated visiting the Grand Canyon. He was scheduled to run a marathon in St. George, Utah, five days after our planned Canyon hike and thought a long walk would be a great prelude to a long run. Always eager to share my love and knowledge of the Canyon, I had no objection to Jim joining Charley and me for the cross-canyon walk. The inclusion of Charley and Jim on this hike increased to twenty the number of people I introduced to Canyon hiking.

We made the long drive from Salina to the South Rim, stopping at Gallup, New Mexico, for the night. From Gallup it was a short drive to Grand Canyon Village, giving us time to stop at many of the scenic overviews along the South Rim. Our first stop along the rim was Desert View. Despite haze caused by forest fires burning on both rims, we had glorious views up and down the Canyon and across the Colorado River to the Unkar Creek drainage.

I wondered how I would describe the Grand Canyon to a blind person. Could words adequately capture the breadth and depth of the Canyon? What words would I use to describe its geographic features and panoply of colors? I could do no better explaining a symphony to a deaf person or the aroma of freshly baked bread to someone without a sense of smell.

I thought about it a little longer. It was unacceptable to evade describing the Grand Canyon to the sightless. Perhaps words were not enough, but what about music? John Wesley Powell said: "The wonders of the Grand Canyon cannot be adequately represented in symbols of speech, nor by speech itself … It is the land of music … a land of song. Mountains of music swell in the rivers, hills of music billow in the creeks, and meadows of music murmur in the rills that ripple over the rocks … All this is the music of the waters." I had the answer. If asked to describe the Grand Canyon to someone without the sense of sight I would have them listen to Grofe's *Grand Canyon Suite* and Paul Winter's *Canyon*. Ferde Grofe completed the *Grand Canyon Suite* in 1931, and it is arguably the best musical portrait of the Canyon. Paul Winter and his Consort recorded *Canyon* in 1980 during a raft trip down the

Colorado River through the Grand Canyon. Paul Winter claims he "barely touched the challenge of translating the spirit of the canyon into sound," but I believe he did paint with musical notes a beautiful picture of the Grand Canyon.

Looking up and down the Canyon and from one rim to the other I pondered on the formation of this magnificent chasm. The simplest explanation for the canyon's creation was advanced by the teller of tall-tales, John Hance, who claimed he dug it, creating the San Francisco Peaks near Flagstaff with the dirt excavated from the big ditch.

Through the years more believable theories have been proposed regarding the genesis of the Grand Canyon. I recently read Wayne Ranney's book, *Carving Grand Canyon*, and found it a concise yet thorough discussion of the various ideas pertaining to the origin of the Colorado River and the Grand Canyon.

Ranney outlined a series of events he believed led to the formation of the Grand Canyon. First, between five hundred forty and eighty million years ago, ancient seas deposited layer upon layer of flat-lying Grand Canyon strata. Younger layers eroded, leaving the Kaibab limestone (deposited two hundred fifty million years ago) at the top. Beneath the Kaibab limestone lie the ten other layers of sedimentary rock recognized today. Between eighty and seventy million years ago the ancient seas withdrew and an initial system of rivers was established in the Grand Canyon region. A broad uplifting of the region called the Mogollon Highlands (now known as the Colorado Plateau) occurred over the next forty million years (seventy to thirty million years ago) resulting in a system of rivers flowing to the northeast. Between thirty and sixteen million years ago gradual lowering of the Mogollon Highlands caused rivers in the area to become ponded, rerouted, or dry. Over the next ten million years lowering of the areas upstream and downstream from what would become the Grand Canyon occurred. Opening of the Gulf of California approximately six million years ago started the process leading to creation of the modern Colorado River flowing to the southwest. By five and a half million years ago a free-flowing Colorado River crossed the Kaibab Plateau. The Grand Canyon deepened and widened by increased Ice Age runoff and erosion of knickpoints (abrupt changes in the longitudinal profile of a stream) that formed in the river along fault zones.

As plausible as this explanation for the formation of the Grand Canyon may seem, the precise sequence of events remains unknown. The mystery surrounding the creation of the Grand Canyon made it all the more attractive to me.

On the afternoon of our arrival at Grand Canyon Village on the South Rim I had the good fortune to meet Shirley Gaudreau, wife of Laurent Gaudreau (a.k.a. Maverick). Shirley worked as a cashier at the Visitors Center Bookstore. She confirmed that her husband had walked across the Canyon over one hundred times in his eightieth year. I asked her if she called him Maverick. "No, I call him sweetheart," she replied. She went on to add that when she got mad at him, she told him to "Go take a hike!" Maverick was still hiking in the Canyon at eighty-three years of age, but not as frequently as three years earlier.*

"Every journey starts with a first step," Charley announced. For this and other bits of wisdom he chose to share, his traveling companions dubbed him The Philosopher. In turn, Charley called me the Hikemeister, as I was the expedition leader and curator of Canyon trivia. In the predawn darkness of Monday, September 29, The Philosopher, The Animal, and The Hikemeister took their first steps down the South Kaibab Trail, using headlamps to illuminate the steep, dusty path. This most amazing day would consist of thousands of steps—nearly fifty thousand steps given my twenty-eight inch stride.

Within an hour and a half we had descended below Cedar Ridge and no longer needed headlamps to see the trail. Recalling that eight hundred three cubic miles of rock were eroded away to form the Grand Canyon, I asked my companions how many dump truck loads of earth would be necessary to fill it to the brim. Jim, a structural engineer, wanted to know what size dump truck would be used. I had no idea. However, remembering that a contactor wheelbarrow held eight cubic feet of earth, I calculated that it would take approximately fifteen trillion (fifteen followed by twelve zeros) wheelbarrow loads to get the job done. If a thousand workmen each dumped one hundred wheelbarrow loads of dirt into the Canyon per day, it would take over 400,000 years to fill it, providing none of it washed away. Where did eight hundred three

<hr>

* On February 5, 2009 Laurent "Maverick" Gaudreau and his wife Shirley were found shot to death in their mobile home on the South Rim in an apparent murder-suicide. According to a shuttle bus driver on the South Rim, Shirley was terminally ill and Maverick could not face life without his wife.

cubic miles of dirt eroded from the Grand Canyon go? According to geologist Wayne Ranney, the soil was deposited in what is now known as the Imperial Valley in Southern California, where the Colorado River once emptied into the Gulf of California. Farmers are growing vegetables in Grand Canyon soil.

Not content to limit my quiz to one question, I proceeded to ask Charley and Jim a variety of questions pertaining to the Grand Canyon. "What are the rock layers of the Canyon?" *Answer*: Kaibab Limestone, Toroweap Formation, Coconino Sandstone, Hermit Shale, Supai Group, Redwall Limestone, Temple Butte Limestone, Muav Limestone, Bright Angel Shale, Tapeats Sandstone, Grand Canyon Supergroup, and Vishnu Schist. "Why is the Colorado River water running through the Grand Canyon so cold?" *Answer*: It comes from the bottom of Lake Powell. "Why did the Colorado River run green rather than brown?" *Answer*: Silt in the river is trapped behind Glen Canyon Dam. "Who named Bright Angel Creek?" *Answer*: Major John Wesley Powell. "How were the rapids of the Colorado River formed?" *Answer*: Boulders were washed into the river from side canyons. "How many bridges would we cross on our trip to the North Rim?" *Answer*: Seven (Kaibab Suspension Bridge, four bridges in The Box, a bridge at the mouth of Roaring Springs Canyon, and a bridge across a dry gap in The Redwall). Needless to say, my pupils performed miserably on their test. Charley did manage to figure out why the Kaibab Suspension Bridge was also called the Black Bridge and how the Silver Bridge got its name.

In contrast to my last crossing in May 2007 prickly pear cacti no longer displayed colorful blooms. Reddish egg-shaped fruit on paddle-shaped stems of the cacti were all that remained of the yellow and red flowers of spring. Century plants were also devoid of blooms. Scattered throughout the Canyon were hundreds of bare spikes, each projecting from a cluster of dried leaves at its base—remnants of last spring's bloom. I asked Charley about the nature of these poles. He was certain they were placed in the Canyon to measure snow depth along the trail. In addition to being the trip philosopher Charley was the trip humorist.

Within a quarter mile of the Colorado River our forward progress was briefly interrupted by mule trains—first a group of mules coming down from the South Rim delivering supplies to Phantom Ranch, and then two groups of mules going up carrying human cargo from Phantom Ranch to the rim. By 8:00 AM, we reached the Kaibab Suspension Bridge (Black Bridge) and crossed the Colorado River, emerald green in the morning light. Charley confirmed that the Black Bridge was indeed black in color. Twenty minutes later we arrived at Phantom Ranch, quiet after discharging overnight visitors a half-hour earlier.

I was concerned about our slow progress from South Rim to Phantom Ranch—a cautious pace dictated by descending the first three miles in the dark and by our aversion to twisting an ankle or straining a knee on the steep downhill grade. Charley reminded me that we were not racing across the Canyon. "We're on a stroll, not a run," he remarked. Nevertheless, I did not want to be caught in the inner canyon during the warmest part of the day. By the time we arrived at Phantom Ranch the sun was well above the rim and within a couple of hours direct sunlight would heat the entire length of North Kaibab Trail coursing through Bright Angel Canyon. If we hustled, we could walk in the shadows of The Box but would miss the opportunity to walk in morning shadows from beyond The Box to Cottonwood.

As expected, we walked in the shade through the narrow passage in The Box. Upon exiting The Box we were greeted by bright sunlight and the warmth it brought—sapping some of the energy I wanted to reserve for the climb to the North Rim. Bothered less by the heat and being in much better physical condition than I, Jim and Charley did not seem concerned about walking in the inner canyon at mid-day.

Above The Box the trail cut through a patch of marshland. On previous trips I had to slosh through this area, often sinking ankle-deep in the muck. Since my last crossing of the Canyon the park service had built an elevated boardwalk through the marsh, protecting the riparian flora from human feet and keeping those feet high and dry.

Upon reaching the start of the climb up of Asinine Hill (six miles from Phantom Ranch) we sighted Ribbon Falls across Bright Angel Creek to the west. I asked Charley and Jim whether they wanted to make a detour to Ribbon Falls or climb the hill and keep on trucking up the trail toward Cottonwood. Jim wanted to make the side trip to Ribbon Falls, even though it added another half mile to our trek and delayed our exit from the Canyon by an hour. Charley wanted to continue toward Cottonwood. I cast the deciding vote. Not knowing whether any of us would come this way again, I voted to go to Ribbon Falls.

Abandoning the trail, we waded across Bright Angel Creek towards the falls. We had avoided soaking our boots in the marsh but keeping them dry crossing Bright Angel Creek proved impossible—there were too few stepping stones above waterline to allow dry passage. On the west side of Bright Angel Creek we slogged along vestigial trails through thick brush towards Ribbon Falls. The extra energy expended bushwhacking to the falls was more than rewarded by the refreshing showers we took in the cold water cascading down the moss-covered cone at its base.

Charley Griffin and Jim Manley crossing Bright
Angel Creek on the way to Ribbon Falls

Reinvigorated by cold showers, consumption of a few calories, and a brief respite from walking, we trudged on, arriving at Cottonwood shortly after noon—eight hours on the trail and two-thirds of the trip done. The thermometer at Cottonwood read ninety degrees. Our luck had held. We would not have to walk in brutal mid-day heat, as it would get cooler as we climbed from Cottonwood to the rim. Although I did not relish the steep climb out of the Canyon, I looked forward to exiting the rapidly warming Bright Angel Canyon and walking in the afternoon shade of the north-facing wall of Roaring Springs Canyon.

Just beyond Roaring Springs we passed a couple from Michigan walking across the Canyon in a day. We first met them at Cottonwood when they stopped to fill their water containers. They left Cottonwood before us, apparently anxious to catch up with the rest of their group, including their two children and the woman's father, who were ahead of them. At Cottonwood they seemed in good spirits and good shape, but by the time they reached the base of the Redwall beyond the turnoff to Roaring Springs the pair had lost the spring in their step. The Canyon had a way of doing that, even to the fit hiker. As we climbed through the Redwall and Supai Formation the distance between them and us progressively lengthened. It did not cross my mind that they might be in trouble.

Traffic seemed lighter than usual on the North Kaibab Trail. We were at the end of the busy season on the North Rim. In addition to the Michigan couple, we encountered only a few small groups of backpackers descending into the Canyon, presumably headed for Cottonwood Campground where they would spend the night before proceeding onward.

I slowly ascended the sinuous trail up to the rim—my progress slow but steady. The climb through the Supai formation did not seem as bad as I remembered from previous trips. Jim and Charley accepted my slow pace—it enabled them to survey and photograph the scenery. Charley, always the sage, reminded me, "If it was easy, anyone could do it!" It certainly was not easy but every walk in the Grand Canyon presented some difficulty.

Within a mile of finishing I told Charley and Jim that we had several more miles of hard climbing to go, hoping to psychologically deflate them. The tactic failed. They were aware of my tendency towards exaggeration, and they also had a good idea of our pace and time on the trail and figured the top was near, although not seen because of dense forest. We reached the trailhead by 5:20 PM—completing the crossing in slightly less than thirteen hours. The Michigan group, waiting for the last two hikers in their group, loudly cheered as we made the last steps to the top—the most rousing finish I had experienced in all my years of Canyon hiking. The feelings of elation at completing the hike were exceeded only by the happiness of starting the journey earlier that morning. Our cheerleaders from Michigan were informed that they would need to wait a good deal longer for the last two members of their party.

Typically, early on the morning following completion of each hike I vacated the Canyon rim in order to start the journey back to Kansas. My routine changed this trip. Jack, John, Charley, and I spent an extra day on the North Rim, eating a leisurely breakfast, lounging on the sunporch of the lodge, and walking out to Bright Angel Point, where I met the father of the Michigan woman Jim, Charley, and I had passed on the trail the previous afternoon. He informed me that his daughter and son-in-law did not make it out until late the previous evening. The woman apparently had become confused as a result of a severe electrolyte imbalance (hyponatremia), presumably caused by water intoxication, and was evacuated by helicopter to Flagstaff for emergency medical treatment. The Canyon did not claim another victim but repeated the warning that hiking in its hallowed walls was not without danger.

Jack wanted to photograph aspens displaying their fall colors, and I wanted to explore the access route to the Nankoweap Trail (U.S.G.S. maps: Point Imperial, Nankoweap Mesa). An excursion out of the park allowed us to do both. We drove a short distance north of the park boundary before turning east on a forest service road cutting through the Saddle Mountain Wilderness Area. The road was lined by groves of brilliant yellow aspens—enough to satisfy Jack's desire.

At the end of a long dirt road we found Forest Service Trail 57, which headed east along the rim for three miles before intersecting the Nankoweap Trail. The Nankoweap Trail was purportedly the most difficult named hiking trail in Grand Canyon; it dipped below the rim and continued another eleven miles through rough terrain to the Colorado River, where it terminated at river mile 52.1.

Major John Wesley Powell and his group originally constructed the trail during an 1882 expedition. The trail followed a Paiute route and allowed the group's geologist, Charles Doolittle Walcott, to examine the Canyon's rock layers from river to rim.

Jack, John, Charley, and I walked only a few hundred yards on the Forest Service trail along the rim. The views from the rim towards Nankoweap Canyon were nothing short of spectacular. I salivated at the idea of hiking down the Nankoweap Trail but realized I was not prepared for such a strenuous trip. Perhaps my son and one or two of his friends could be enticed to accompany me on the trip—and carry much of the load.

Colin Fletcher exited the Grand Canyon using the Nankoweap Trail on his epic trek in 1963 recorded in his book *The Man Who Walked Through Time*. If not the spiritual godfather of backpacking, he was certainly among the founding brethren. In 1989 Fletcher hiked and rafted the entire length of the Green/Colorado River system from its source in the Wind River Range in Wyoming to its termination at the Gulf of California. Once again his journey took him through the Grand Canyon, albeit by boat. He published his story in 1997 in the book *River*. Like previous books, *River* was more than an adventure story. Traveling down the river was a metaphor of life from conception to death. Like life, the river ran smooth at times and at other times was turbulent; obstacles were introduced and periods of pure joy were experienced. Colin Fletcher's life journey ended on June 19, 2007. He died from complications of a head injury suffered six years earlier when he was hit by a motor vehicle while walking to a meeting near his home in northern California.

Sitting on the sun porch of Grand Canyon Lodge, watching the sun slowly set over the Canyon, I recalled the celebrated Grand Canyon hikers who shared my love for this place—John Wesley Powell, Harvey Butchart, George Steck, and Colin Fletcher. Surely during the past forty-seven years I had walked on the same ground that they had trod. I looked down into the depths of the Canyon and across to the South Rim and was once again amazed that I had actually walked across this grandest of canyons. However, more rewarding than hiking across the Canyon in one day were the bonds of friendship strengthened during the trip. Charley, Jack, John, and I spent six days together on this Grand Canyon trip—discussing politics and religion, telling tall tales, sharing meals, and keeping each other up at night with loud snoring. The humor and wisdom each of my friends imparted were hard to summarize—like trying to describe the Grand Canyon to someone who has not seen it.

Chapter 18
Winter in the Canyon

January 2010

> *... so I trudge on down the foggy road of life,*
> *trying to fill up my days, knowing I won't see them twice.*
> *Many years from now when just a stone marks where I lay,*
> *Know that I was here, if only for a day.*

> **—Chris Beck, singer, songwriter, and friend,**
> **from his song "Take Me Back"**

Starting a hike in the Grand Canyon always generates a little anxiety. Am I in good enough shape for the hike planned? Are my hiking companions physically and mentally prepared? Will it be too hot? Too cold? Will I carry enough food and water? What new could be thrown my way? This trip would be no different, especially when it was my first winter hike in the Canyon.

I had never hiked in the Grand Canyon during the winter months. Spring, summer, and fall, yes. Winter, no. A winter hike was on my bucket list, but winter at the Grand Canyon posed new challenges—cold, rather than hot weather, snow and ice on trails in the higher elevations, fewer people on the trail in case emergency assistance was needed. Nevertheless, my story could not be completed without a winter trip to the Canyon. Since access to the North Rim was limited during winter months, I needed to confine my walk to South Rim routes. Once again, my good friend John Divine volunteered to accompany me to the Canyon.

For my first winter walk I chose a loop hike—down the South Kaibab Trail to the Tonto Trail, west on the Tonto Trail to Indian Garden, and up the Bright Angel Trail to the South Rim—a distance of 13.5 miles. We chose not to camp in the Canyon, preferring to stay in comfortable lodging on the rim before and after the long walk.

John Divine on icy South Kaibab Trail

John and I started down the South Kaibab Trail shortly after sunrise on Monday, January 11, 2010. The temperature hovered near thirty

152

degrees and the sky was devoid of clouds. Compared to the minus ten degrees we had experienced in Kansas two days earlier, it was downright balmy. I saw snow as far down as the Muav layer on the north facing walls of Pipe Creek Canyon, while on the south facing walls of the North Rim snow could not be seen below the Kaibab Limestone.

A four- to six-inch layer of packed snow or ice covered the upper stretch of the trail. The upper canyon took on a different appearance with a winter coat of snow; large patches of white were interspersed with the reds, pinks, yellows and browns of the rock walls. We strapped on instep crampons and carefully started down the trail. Trekking poles were used to assist with stability on the slick trail. I wore four layers of clothes on my upper body and two layers on my legs, even though I knew it would not take me long to warm up.

Just above Cedar Ridge we met a couple leaving the Canyon. They had tried to complete a rim to river and back trip the day before (down the Bright Angel Trail and up the South Kaibab Trail) but managed to make it out only as far as Cedar Ridge before darkness fell, halting upward progress. Fortunately they carried a tent and sleeping bags; otherwise they would have had to seek overnight shelter in a composting toilet at Cedar Ridge.

At the base of O'Neill Butte we walked out of the ice and snow and were able to remove our crampons and a couple layers of clothing, and quicken our pace. Above Skeleton Point we met a National Park Service work crew repairing damage to the trail caused by mule traffic. They were crushing rocks with a new rock crusher brought in by helicopter. The walnut-sized gravel produced by the crusher was then shoveled into the large divots in the trail caused by mule trains. The rangers said that mule traffic was banned from the trail for four years, during which time the trail would undergo extensive repairs. They hoped the refurbished trail would withstand the damaging effects of mule hooves.

Just above the Redwall four young men running to the Colorado River passed John and me. I had been walking for over two hours and they had covered the same distance in forty minutes. Once they reached the river they planned to return to the rim via the Bright Angel Trail. They wore shorts, long sleeve shirts, and running shoes, and each carried a single water bottle; sweaters, jackets, and crampons were not evident. Perhaps they had skated down the icy trail above us.

As we descended the Redwall we passed two more NPS trail repair crews. Instead of using crushed rock, they were constructing a cobblestone trail by fitting together large flat-sided stones. It appeared to be an incredibly tedious and backbreaking job. I wondered how many feet of trail they could pave in a day.

Four and a half miles from the rim the South Kaibab Trail intercepted the Tonto Trail. The path between the South Kaibab Trail and Indian Garden was level and narrow—blackbush scrub lining the trail grabbed at my pants legs and trekking poles. The sky was a brilliant blue and the temperature was a comfortable fifty-six degrees. After walking west a short distance, we veered south towards the head of Pipe Creek Canyon, crossing Burro Springs on the way. Burro Springs was not much more than a narrow marsh.

Water flowed in Pipe Creek but it was not much deeper than the soles of my boots. Pipe Creek derived its name from a Meerschaum pipe Ralph Cameron found lying in the streambed in 1894 while traveling across the Tonto Plateau ahead of his brother Niles and two other miners. Apparently Ralph etched a date about one hundred years previous on it and placed it where the rest of his party would find it. Upon discovering the pipe, Ralph's companions speculated as to who had been there so long before, much to the delight of Ralph. John and I found no interesting artifacts in the streambed on our trip. After crossing Pipe Creek the route turned northwest towards Garden Creek and intercepted the Bright Angel Trail.

Instead of the usually bustling way station between rim and river during spring, summer, and fall, Indian Garden in winter was as quiet as a snowfall, except there was no snow on the ground. The few leaves still clinging to the branches of the cottonwoods lining Garden Creek were a dull brown. Only the green of cacti and the blue of the sky added color to the scene. I extracted a camping stove and a small pot from my daypack and boiled water for a late lunch of soup and hot chocolate.

John did not need to tell me he was tired. I could see the look of fatigue on his face. Food, fluids, and rest did not erase that guise. Not prepared to spend the night in the Canyon, John and I had no choice but to climb the final 4.5 miles to the rim—or spend the night in an outhouse.

In contrast to literally hundreds of hikers on the trail between Indian Garden and the rim during the spring, summer, and fall seasons, I counted no more than a half dozen brave souls this winter afternoon. I silently sang the old gospel song "We Are Climbing Jacob's Ladder" as I climbed the series of switchbacks in The Redwall known as Jacob's Ladder. Every rung went higher, higher. There were enough switchbacks to repeat the verses several times.

At the Three-Mile Resthouse the trail became too slick to proceed without crampons. The trail was an icy chute—like a bobsled run. John was tiring, and by the One-and-Half-Mile Resthouse I had lost contact with him. I waited at the resthouse for fifteen minutes—still no John. Down the trail I went, finding him a switchback below me. John reassured me that he was okay and would make it to the top and implored me to proceed at my on speed without him. I told him we would climb out together at a pace set by him, which turned out to be painfully slow—ten steps, then rest a few seconds, and then another ten steps. Twilight turned to darkness. Fortunately, even in the dark, it was easy to follow the trail cut in the snow. Finally, thirty minutes after complete darkness enveloped the Canyon, we reached Kolb Studio. John was spent. After a hot shower he crawled into bed and stayed there for twelve hours. Before falling asleep he told me that the day's walk was two miles too long and that the soup I fed him for lunch contributed to his distress. However, he was grateful that he did not have to climb out of the canyon alone.

By the next morning John had recovered but expressed no interest in another long walk. I had hoped to make a second winter foray into the Canyon—a three-mile walk down the Grandview Trail to Horseshoe Mesa. Horseshoe Mesa was perched on The Redwall halfway between rim and river, and from above looked like a horseshoe attached to the end of a peninsula jutting out from the South Rim. The open end of the horseshoe pointed north, towards the Colorado River.

Grandview Trail was an old Indian route improved in 1892–93 by Pete Berry and several other miners to reach The Last Chance Mine on Horseshoe Mesa. During the early and middle 1890s a considerable amount of high-grade copper was hauled out of the mines on Horseshoe Mesa. The mines were closed in 1907 when expenses exceeded revenues garnered from the operation.

In addition to mining Pete Berry operated a hotel at Grandview Point. The Grandview Hotel was a two-story lodge built in 1897 of native ponderosa pines. It served visitors to the Canyon until 1907. In 1905 the Santa Fe Railroad completed construction of the El Tovar Hotel near their train station on the South Rim, eleven miles to the west of Grandview Point. The Grandview Hotel could not compete with a superior accommodation in a premier location.

A National Park Service ranger at the Visitors Center said the upper Grandview Trail was a nightmare due to its steepness and ice and snow on the trail. Two rangers we later met at Indian Garden said it could be done, if we wore crampons and used trekking poles. They would not go so far as to call it a nightmare. At the very least I wanted to investigate the trailhead and walk down the trail a short distance. John and I drove east of Grand Canyon Village to Grandview Point and the start of the trail (7,420 feet in elevation). It was too steep and icy for John, and after his difficulties of the previous day I agreed that he had no business trying it.

The trail was not a nightmare—only a bad dream. John had no problem with my going on alone, especially since three seasoned hikers had just started down the trail ahead of me and were returning by the same route after they explored Horseshoe Mesa. Promising John—and myself—to keep this group ahead of me on the way down and behind me on the way out, I grabbed water, food, crampons and trekking poles and headed out. John said he would be back at the trailhead in four hours.

"It might be five hours," I replied.

A sign at the trailhead said the trail was "steep, steep, steep." I would add a "very" to that. The Grandview Trail (U.S.G.S. maps: Grandview Point, Cape Royal) was among the steepest I had hiked in the Canyon. In addition to being steep, it was covered by deep snow that had been packed into a fourteen-inch wide, eight to twelve inch deep trough. Occasionally I would plant my trekking pole on the outside edge of the trail only to have it sink to the hilt without hitting solid ground—not a good place to step. The trail wasted no time getting to the Supai Formation—quickly dropping through the Kaibab, Toroweap, Coconino, and Hermit Shale layers in a succession of switchbacks.

In the upper Coconino layer the snow had melted, exposing a short stretch of the cobblestone trail laid down by Pete Berry in the early 1890s. I removed my crampons, only to find more ice and snow a few switchbacks lower. I reattached the crampons to my boots.

The trail made a lengthy traverse through the Supai on the east wall of upper Cottonwood Creek Canyon. The route leveled in the Supai but the snow and ice persisted for another half-mile. I began to wonder whether Horseshoe Mesa could be reached in the self-imposed time limit of two hours for the outbound trip.

I arrived at Pete Berry's Last Chance Mine with five minutes to spare. The remnants of his cabin on Horseshoe Mesa lie a few hundred yards to the north. The three hikers that had preceded me down the trail could neither be seen nor heard. Had they hiked out to one end or the other of the horseshoe or had they decided to descend the Redwall to the east to Miner's Spring or the Redwall to the west towards Cottonwood Creek? Exploration of the mesa beckoned, but I needed to head back, knowing it would take me at least two, if not three hours to return to the rim.

After a quick lunch I started the uphill trek. The trail was just as steep going uphill as downhill—and the going was slower. I had to be careful climbing on the ice and snow—making sure each foot plant had purchase. This was definitely work for me and would have been troublesome for John—perhaps the nightmare a ranger had described. My heart pounded. My lungs screamed for more air. The silence of my winter walk was interrupted only by the crunch of ice and snow underfoot, my breathing, and the cry of a few ravens flying near the rim. I was thankful that it was winter and I could keep cool by removing a layer of clothes.

I reached the rim three hours after starting my uphill climb, finding John patiently waiting for me. Unlike most of my hikes in the Canyon during spring, summer, and fall, I saw no humans from rim to mesa to rim. Although tired, I was ready for a good meal; sleep could wait.

This trip marked nearly fifty years of hiking in Grand Canyon—approximately five hundred horizontal miles and sixty days below the rim—nowhere near the miles hiked and time spent in the Canyon by Harvey Butchart or George Steck. My labors in the Grand Canyon are not extraordinary. Multiple individuals have numbers more impressive than mine. I realized my time in the Canyon was more than numbers—days below the rim, miles hiked, switchbacks negotiated, stream crossings, walking speed, pounds in my pack—although I have obsessively recorded these statistics. Conquering the Canyon—an unobtainable and foolish quest—ceased to be a goal. I returned to the Canyon because of what it did for me, not what I could do in it.

I cherished memories of canyon colors, smells along the trail, good and bad meals, nights spent on the ground falling asleep under a magnificent sky framed by canyon walls, the rumble of river rapids, the roar of Roaring Springs and Thunder Springs, the rushing, crystal clear water of Bright Angel Creek, the distinctive descending call of canyon wrens, the companionship of many friends, and quietly walking alone. I have learned a little about the Grand Canyon in nearly fifty years—its geology, plants and animals, and its human history. I have learned how to survive for short periods of time in the Canyon—what time of day to walk, and when not to walk, how much water to carry, what to bring in my pack. Fortunately, I never suffered an injury or serious illness in the Canyon. Most importantly, I learned something about myself—my ability to persevere despite discomfort, my need to spend time in the wild, and my need for a time of silence in nature.

I have spent time in other grand canyons—Bryce, Zion, and Waimea, the Grand Canyon of Hawaii on Kauai. Although each is beautiful and unique, in my opinion they pale in comparison to the Grand Canyon of Arizona. Size does make a difference—and then add the Colorado River, multiple side canyons, the age of rocks exposed, and the variety of climate zones. The Grand Canyon is beyond compare. I am called to walk in the king of canyons.

Perhaps, as long as I could hike in Grand Canyon I fooled myself into believing I was not getting old, although trying to prove I could still do it made me old, not young. Hiking in the Canyon afforded me the opportunity to get away from schedules and the daily routine and immerse myself in the ancient rhythms. Trips to the Canyon reconnected me to all of creation and reinforced my desire to preserve the natural beauty of the earth for future generations. The Canyon was truly a sanctuary, a sanitarium, a place of healing. After each hike in the Grand Canyon I wondered if I would return. Once my tired legs, sore and stiff joints, and bruised toes healed I started thinking about another hike. Why did I do it? I guess because I needed the tonic the Canyon offered.

Appendix A

Grand Canyon Geology

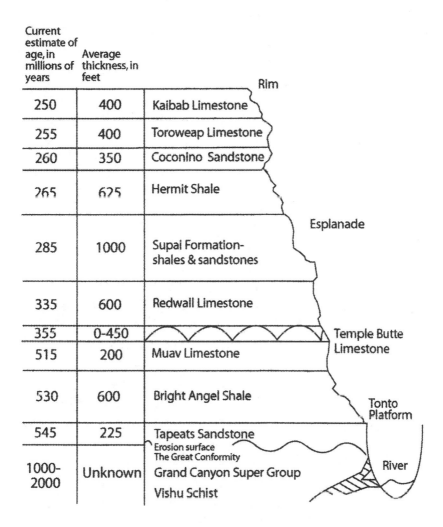

Current estimate of age, in millions of years	Average thickness, in feet		
			Rim
250	400	Kaibab Limestone	
255	400	Toroweap Limestone	
260	350	Coconino Sandstone	
265	625	Hermit Shale	
			Esplanade
285	1000	Supai Formation- shales & sandstones	
335	600	Redwall Limestone	
355	0-450		Temple Butte Limestone
515	200	Muav Limestone	
530	600	Bright Angel Shale	Tonto Platform
545	225	Tapeats Sandstone	
		Erosion surface The Great Conformity	
1000-2000	Unknown	Grand Canyon Super Group	River
		Vishu Schist	

Appendix B
Thirteen Essentials for Hiking in Grand Canyon

Fail to plan, plan to fail!

**—Proverbial saying, often preached by
my friend Paul Edstrom.**

During the past fifty years I have observed many changes in the realm of hiking and camping. More people are on the trail, especially in the Grand Canyon. Many wilderness areas are not so wild anymore. A half-century ago one did not worry about contaminated stream water. Now we are implored to filter or treat water from even the most pristine of streams for fear of developing giardiasis, hepatitis, or another equally dreadful illness. The canvas pup tent, metal canteen, and packboard are extinct. Through the years quantum leaps in the quality, durability, and functionality of camping and backpacking equipment and clothing have occurred. Lightweight, high-tech products have proliferated—custom-fitted backpacks, lighter, warmer sleeping bags, puncture-resistant sleeping pads, water and wind-shedding tents, fuel-efficient stoves that fit in the palm of your hand, water filters/purifiers, and functional yet stylish clothing. Of course, none of this equipment is cheap. Nevertheless, proper preparation and equipment cannot be ignored if you are planning a walk in Grand Canyon.

In the 1930s, The Mountaineers, a Seattle-based organization for climbers and outdoor adventurers, compiled a list of indispensable equipment for a backpacking trip—the Ten Essentials. The original list has been updated in the 2003 edition of the book, *Mountaineering: The Freedom of the Hills.* The updated Ten Essentials list included: (1) navigation; (2) sun protection; (3) insulation (extra clothing); (4) illumination; (5) first-aid supplies; (6) fire; (7) repair kit and tools; (8) nutrition (extra food); (9) hydration (extra water); and (10) emergency shelter.

I gratefully acknowledge The Mountaineers' important contribution to backcountry adventure preparedness. I have expanded and customized their list, creating a list of essentials for hiking in the Grand Canyon—a list I call The Thirteen Essentials: (1) physical preparation; (2) common sense/safety; (3) proper footwear and clothing; (4) walking staff or trekking poles; (5) day pack/backpack; (6) water; (7) food and fire; (8) shelter; (9) sleeping bag and pad; (10) illumination; (11) first aid kit; (12) repair kit and tools; and (13) miscellaneous items.

PHYSICAL PREPARATION

Preparing one's body for a physically challenging hike is of primary importance. Participation in a program of regular exercise, including walking up and down steps or hills, is paramount to readying oneself for the hike. The Grand Canyon is no place to try out Professor Harold Hill's "think system." Before taking a long hike in Grand Canyon, test out your legs, heart, and lungs on a short stretch of a main corridor trail. Your first trek should not be an attempt to walk from rim-to-river and back in one day or to cross the Canyon in one day. If you have any doubts about your physical ability to take a long walk in the Grand Canyon, *DO NOT GO*, or consult your physician before going. If you are planning a long walk, start training at least six months in advance. At the same time, make reservations for lodging on the rims, if needed, as lodging is limited and fills quickly.

In the appendix to his guidebook, *Hiking Grand Canyon National Park*, Ron Adkison lists a wide variety of hikes, ranging from day hikes and overnighters suitable for families to hikes "for backpackers who think they have seen it all, demanding routes that stretch the meaning of the word 'trail'." It is imperative that the distance and difficulty of the hike not exceed the abilities of the weakest hiker in your group.

COMMON SENSE

Any hike in Grand Canyon should be guided by common sense. The Canyon hiker using common sense adequately prepares for the trip, never attempts a longer hike than he or she is physically prepared to complete, never hikes in the wilderness areas of Canyon alone, carries an ample amount of food and water, wears appropriate clothing and footwear, never ignores the early warning signs of fatigue and dehydration during the trip, and remains calm when faced with a challenge. The Grand Canyon is unforgiving and no place for an impulsive, foolhardy hiker. When planning a hike in the Grand Canyon, be aware of the climate conditions you may encounter (see following tables), and before leaving on your hike, obtain an up-to-date weather report.

South Rim Averages			
Month	High (F)	Low (F)	Precipitation (inches)
January	41	18	1.3
February	45	21	1.5
March	51	25	1.4
April	60	32	0.9
May	70	39	0.7
June	81	47	0.4
July	84	54	1.8
August	82	53	2.2
September	76	47	1.6
October	65	36	1.1
November	52	27	0.9
December	43	20	1.6

Inner Canyon Averages

Month	High (F)	Low (F)	Precipitation (inches)
January	56	36	0.7
February	62	42	0.8
March	71	48	0.8
April	82	56	0.5
May	92	63	0.4
June	101	72	0.3
July	106	78	0.8
August	103	75	1.4
September	97	69	1.0
October	84	58	0.6
November	68	46	0.4
December	57	37	0.9

North Rim Averages

Month	High (F)	Low (F)	Precipitation (inches)
January	37	16	3.2
February	39	18	3.2
March	44	21	2.6
April	53	29	1.7
May	62	34	1.2
June	72	40	0.9
July	77	46	1.9
August	75	45	2.8
September	69	39	2.0
October	59	31	1.4
November	46	24	1.5
December	40	20	2.8

During the summer months, hike during the cooler hours of the day (early to mid-morning and late afternoon to evening); rest in the shade when the sun is high in the sky. During the winter months, be aware that the upper stretches of many trails may be snow-packed or icy and that hours of daylight are much less.

On the rims, never climb over guardrails or guard walls. They are there to protect you from falling into the abyss. There may be a sheer cliff or unstable rock beyond the wall or rail. According to Michael Ghiglieri and Tom Myers in their book *Over the Edge: Death in Grand Canyon*, of the fifty deaths from falls from the rims, many were victims of stupidity, including ten that were posing for or taking pictures.

It is also advisable to stick to the established trail. A shortcut can damage vulnerable foliage and dislodge rocks that may injure hikers below you. A shortcut can also lead to an impassable cliff or blind alley, mandating retracing of steps and expenditure of extra energy, often at time when energy stores are low, the temperature in the Canyon is unbearably hot, and water supplies are dwindling.

If you are hiking in wilderness areas, it is absolutely imperative to research the area before leaving, and take a map, compass, or GPS on the trip. Off-trail hiking in wilderness areas is for experts only. It is best if you travel with someone who has knowledge of the area. Multiple cases of life-threatening heat stroke and death have occurred in the Canyon when hikers became lost.

When hiking in wilderness areas, avoid camping in drainages prone to flash flooding.

Be careful where you place your hands or feet, especially when hiking off trail. You do not want to blindly place your leg or hand near a venomous snake, move a rock or limb under which a scorpion may be hiding, or grab hold of or brush a bare leg against a spiny cactus. Never walk barefoot in the Canyon, and shake out your shoes and socks each morning before putting them on.

When in camp, do not leave your pack or food unattended. Place all foodstuffs in one of the metal boxes provided at many of the campsites along the main corridor trails, or place food in a stuff sack and hang it from a branch of a nearby tree to keep it out of reach from camp marauders. Make every attempt to store packs off the ground too. Any food or food residue in a pack is an invitation for a rodent to gnaw through the fabric to sample the goodies (believe me, I have been victimized!).

Before leaving on a wilderness trip, inform a friend or relative of the dates of your hike and proposed route, and inform this contact person of your exit from the Canyon after completing your trip.

Make a list of everything you need to take for your trip, and check it twice before starting down the trail.

FOOTWEAR AND CLOTHING

Wearing the correct clothing and footwear can make all the difference in the world in terms of comfort on the trail and in camp. Footwear and clothing must be tailored to the type of hike planned and the season of the year in which it is made. If you are making a short day hike during the warmer months of the year, carrying only a lightweight daypack, and confining your walk to a maintained trail, a sturdy pair of walking shoes or mountain runners will suffice. Low-cut footwear provides minimal protection from ankle roll, and on muddy routes or trails across sand or gravel, it is difficult to keep debris out of your shoes. If a long hike is planned, especially over rough terrain, and you anticipate carrying a heavy load, I argue that a sturdy pair of high-cut hiking boots that provide excellent foot and ankle support is imperative. During late fall, winter, and early spring, snow and ice may be encountered on the trail, especially near the rim. Boots and crampons are advised if these conditions exist.

Walking or running shoes can be purchased at almost any shoe store, but you may need to visit a purveyor of backpacking/adventure gear to find a good pair of hiking boots. To complement your hiking boots or shoes, purchase a pair of high-quality, lightweight backpacking socks that will wick moisture away from your feet. Midweight backpacking socks or mountaineering socks are not necessary for warm weather hikes in the Canyon.

Whether taking a short day hike in the Canyon, crossing the Canyon in a day, or planning a multi-day backpacking trip, you must anticipate sun exposure and a wide spectrum of temperatures when you select clothing. It can be very chilly on the rim when you start your hike, become progressively warmer as you hike into the canyon, be insufferably hot in the inner canyon during the mid day hours, and turn cool in the evening in the canyon or upon hiking back to the rim. I recommend layering lightweight synthetic clothing with ultraviolet protection factor (UPF). Wear supportive undergarments that wick moisture away from your skin.

Unless you are confining your walk to warmer hours of the day, when shorts are appropriate, long pants of lightweight but sturdy material will keep your legs warm, protect them from the sun's rays, and, if hiking through brush, protect your skin from nasty scratches. Hikers who prefer to walk in shorts during the warmer hours should consider investing in a pair of convertible pants. Convertible pants allow you to remove the leggings from the upper portion of the trousers, transforming long pants to shorts by simply unzipping the leggings and storing them in your pocket or pack. Wearing convertible pants eliminates the need to carry an extra pair of pants in your pack. Avoid hiking in jeans; they are heavy, warm, and dry slowly when wet.

The keyword for clothing during a winter hike in the Canyon is layering. During my winter hike I started out on the rim wearing four layers over my torso and two on my legs. Specifically, I wore a long-sleeved undershirt, a long-sleeved shirt, a fleece sweater, and a windbreaker. I wore a pair of long underwear bottoms and my nylon convertible pants on my legs. My winter garb was completed with a pair of gloves and a stocking cap. As I walked down the trail and the Canyon temperature rose, I would remove a layer and put it in my daypack. I brought along a pair of gaiters in case I encountered more than a couple of inches of unpacked snow.

During the warmer months I prefer to hike in a short-sleeved, moisture-wicking shirt. A light color will tend to reflect sunlight, while a dark color will absorb the sun's warmth. I recommend a light-colored shirt for warm-season hiking in Grand Canyon. If the air temperature will not exceed seventy degrees Fahrenheit or if you are subject to sunburn, you may consider a long-sleeved shirt constructed of lightweight wicking material. To ward off the chill in the morning and evening hours, try a lightweight polypro sweater. If it is going to be just a bit chillier or there is a chance of rain, a lightweight, water-repelling rain jacket/windbreaker can be included in your gear. Unless you are hiking in the Canyon during the colder winter months, it is not necessary to carry a heavy fleece sweater, down vest, and/or mountain parka. Resist the urge to pack more clothing than you need—an extra pair of undershorts and socks may be all that is necessary. Check the weather forecast before entering the Canyon and plan accordingly.

To protect your head and neck from the brutal sun—and to keep you cooler—wear a broad-brimmed, light-colored hat. Baseball caps are popular headgear but do not protect the ears and back of the neck from the sun. Also, bring along a pair of sunglasses to block 100 percent of ultraviolet light. Don't forget to bring along plenty of sunscreen with a SPF reading of fifteen or higher that blocks UVA and UVB. A severe sunburn will ruin your trip, damage your skin, and increase your chances for skin cancer.

If you are subject to cold hands when walking in the cool morning or evening hours or when lounging around camp on a cool evening, take along a lightweight pair of cotton gardening gloves. You can purchase them in your local hardware or garden store; they will keep your hands warm, can be used to handle hot pots when cooking, and are easy to wash. Likewise, if your head tends to get cold, pack a lightweight stocking cap. More substantial gloves and headwear may be necessary during winter months.

WALKING STAFF AND TREKKING POLES

I am a big advocate of using a walking staff or trekking poles. Whether I am out for a day hike or carrying a heavy pack for several days, I take my trekking poles. Proper use of a hiking staff or trekking poles can take some of the load off your legs. It is estimated that trekking poles can reduce the weight on your legs by as much as 15 percent, distributing it to your arms and shoulders. Trekking poles can also improve your stability on rough terrain or when wading across a stream, add thrust during ascents, and assist in maintaining an upright posture while walking. Trekking poles are absolutely mandatory if you are hiking on snow and ice. If you tend to develop blisters on your hands from gripping trekking poles, try wearing a pair of cycling gloves that can be purchased at a full-service bicycle shop.

DAYPACKS AND BACKPACKS

If you are planning a short day trip in the Canyon or walking across the Canyon in a day, you will need to take along a pack to carry a sweater or windbreaker, sunscreen, sunglasses, camera, water, and food.

I recommend a small daypack such as those that can be purchased at many sporting goods stores, camping supply stores, and backpacking/wilderness adventure stores. I suggest selecting a pack that has padded shoulder straps and allows for adequate airflow between pack and your back. The size of the main compartment can vary, depending on the load you plan on carrying. Many of these packs have a separate inside pocket in which to place a hydration system, such as those marketed by CamelBak or Platypus, and one or more outer pockets to place smaller items, such as cameras, sunscreen, sunglasses, and food items.

The longer the trip planned, the bigger the pack you will need. I strongly recommend professional assistance when selecting a backpack. It is of paramount importance that a pack fit properly. Specifically, the pack must be long enough (from top of shoulder harness to waist belt) to fit your torso length. Fitting a pack is like fitting shoes—one size does not fit all—and an ill-fitting pack will be just as uncomfortable as ill-fitting shoes. A trained salesperson at a reputable backpacking/adventure gear store can provide invaluable assistance selecting a pack that fits your body and fits your needs.

The two types of backpacks available are internal-frame packs and external-frame packs. The choice between the two is often a matter of personal preference. For the first thirty years of backpacking, I carried an external-frame pack, and since the early 1990s, I have predominately carried an internal-frame pack. Frequently, backpackers prefer an external-frame pack for carrying heavy loads on long treks on maintained trails, while an internal-frame pack is chosen for outings across rougher country. External-frame packs are typically more bulky but less expensive than internal-frame packs. Internal-frame packs generally provide more maneuverability, stability, and adjustability than external-frame packs, but are warmer to carry because they ride close to your back. Whatever type of pack you choose, it is important that it have comfortable shoulder straps that won't slip off your shoulders and a waist belt that will distribute a portion of the load to your pelvic bones. If inclement weather is a concern, purchase a rain cover for your pack.

WATER

Nothing will get you into trouble faster than not carrying enough water for your walk in Grand Canyon, especially during the hot summer months (May through September). You should drink at least one quart or liter of fluid for each hour spent hiking in the Canyon. If you do not have ready access to this amount of water in the Canyon—and it is rare that you will—you will need to carry it. This may require carrying four to five quarts of fluid for a six- to eight-mile hike. If there are no guaranteed water sources for two to three days at a stretch, it will be necessary to carry several gallons of water. Remembering that "a pint is a pound the world around," three gallons of water will weigh in at twenty-four pounds, quite a load in addition to other gear that must be carried. You may not need to drink quite as much water on a winter trip, but you will need water. Do not count on the availability of snow as a water source.

Drinking water is available at rest stops and campgrounds along the Bright Angel and North Kaibab Trails but is unavailable on the South Kaibab Trail. Along the main corridor trail water can also be obtained from Pipe Creek and Indian Creek on the south side of the Colorado River, from the river, and from Bright Angel Creek on the north side of the river. However, water obtained from these sources should be boiled, filtered, or treated with iodine tablets before consumption. Outside the main corridor area, drinking water sources are more unpredictable and widely scattered. Never start a hike in Grand Canyon without knowing how much water you will need and the location of the water sources along your route!

I carry either a two or three liter CamelBak hydration system plus two or more one-liter bottles. The safety of plastic bottles containing bisphenol A (BPA) is a subject of debate, although the FDA claims they present no health hazard. If concerned about BPA, use lightweight stainless-steel water bottles. My CamelBak reservoir is safely tucked away and insulated in my pack. I access the water in the reservoir by means of an attached plastic tube with mouthpiece. Once I have emptied the reservoir I consume the water in the bottles.

For trips in the backcountry, where there are long stretches without water sources, you may need to carry extra water and cache it for the uphill trip out. I carry one-gallon plastic containers of drinking water (well marked with my name and the date), hide them along the trail, and record in a notebook exactly where I have placed them.

Never trust the purity of stream, river, spring, or pothole water in the Canyon; they can be contaminated with *Giardia lamblia*, Cryptospridium, *Campylobacter jejuni*, or Hepatitis A. Water should be boiled, treated with iodine tablets, or filtered with a commercially available water filter or purifier before consumption. Filters trap protozoa (1-300 microns in size) and bacteria (0.1-10 microns). Purifiers trap or kill viruses (0.05-0.1 microns) in addition to protozoa and bacteria. On backcountry trips I now carry a small portable water purifier, as it removes viral contaminates in addition to bacteria and giardia. I also throw in a backup supply of iodine tablets, just in case my purifier malfunctions.

FOOD AND FIRE

A Canyon hiker needs fuel—nutrition—to keep hiking. The choice of foods taken is a personal decision, but a variety of high calorie foods—mainly carbohydrates—are recommended. The amount of food packed depends on the length of the trip. For daytrips a simple sack lunch may suffice, as long as it will not spoil in the heat. For multi-day trips, more thought should be given to meals carried. Breakfasts can be as simple as water, reconstituted energy drinks, dried fruit, cereal or granola bars, and bagels, or as complicated as hot tea, coffee or chocolate, hot cereal, scrambled eggs, and pancakes. Suggestions for lunch on the trail include nuts, dried fruit, hard candy, energy bars, crackers, beef jerky, foil pouches of tuna, water, and energy drinks. Evening meals can be a repeat of lunch fare or can be very elaborate, depending on your tastes, the amount of fuel you want to carry, and how much weight and bulk you wish to carry. On multi-day treks hikers frequently depend on lightweight, dehydrated dinners either prepared at home or purchased at backpacking stores. Prepare and taste-test meals at home before the trip. Nothing is worse than working up a voracious appetite on a long hike and finding the food you brought is unappetizing and barely edible.

Most hikers camping in the Canyon will need to boil water for meals, although it is acceptable to carry ready-to-eat, nonperishable foods and avoid cooking. If you want to prepare hot meals or drinks, you will need to carry a stove, fuel, and the necessary utensils to prepare your food. There are a variety of small, lightweight stoves offered to the backpacking cook. My favorite stove, a SVEA 123R, made by Optimus, was purchased in 1973. It does require a little tinkering to get it started and maintenance to keep it running, but it still performs admirably. The base of the SVEA stove is a built-in reservoir for white gas (enough to last seventy-five minutes). The stove will boil a liter of water in seven minutes. For long trips I take along a fuel flask containing additional white gas—the volume depending on the length of the trip and the number of meals I plan to prepare. In lieu of, or in addition to my SVEA stove, I may take a tiny MSR Pocket Rocket stove, weighing in at a mere three ounces. The nozzle can be mounted on a pressurized canister of fuel (isobutane); eight ounces of fuel is enough to boil sixteen liters of water. Do not forget waterproof matches! Your stove is useless if you cannot light it.

Cookware is manufactured from a variety of materials including titanium, aluminum and steel. Titanium is the lightest material but is more expensive than aluminum and steel. Aluminum is lightweight, rugged, and cheap, while steel is heavier and more rugged.

I typically plan on serving meals that require no more than one large pot (with lid) and a frying pan for preparation. I have a four-quart titanium cook pot and a large aluminum fry pan that work great for a group of four to six people. If I plan on a multi-course meal, I will carry an extra two-quart pot. I also carry a large serving spoon to stir the pot and use a cup to serve its contents. Make sure to take along something to pick up hot pots and pans such as a pot lifter and/or glove.

My personal eating utensils consist of a Lexan bowl and cup, a spoon, and a fork—leave the plate and knife at home (use your pocketknife). I pack a nylon-net scrubbing pad and a small plastic container of biodegradable soap to wash dishes. Dishes should be washed and rinsed one hundred feet away from streams.

SHELTER/TENT

A tent will provide warmth and protection from the wind, rain, snow, and insects, and provide a modicum of privacy from neighboring campers. Depending on the time of year you hike in the Canyon, you may not need protection from rain or snow. Check the weather forecast for the dates of your trip before leaving your tent on the rim. If the forecast calls for clear skies and warm temperatures, but you prefer to keep insects at bay and want a refuge in a crowded campground, pack a tent but consider leaving the rainfly behind. The size of the tent depends on the number of people sharing it. For weight-conserving purposes, I recommend that one tent be carried for every two to three people. Two- and three-person tents are typically lightweight and compact, and the tent, fly, poles, guys, and stakes can be easily divided among those using it. Tents for four or more people are typically heavier and bulkier to carry.

Pick a tent with a bathtub floor constructed of tear-resistant fabric. I also advise choosing a tent that is self-standing once erected, as it is often difficult, if not impossible, to stake tent corners and secure guy lines on the rock floor of the Canyon. If all you require is shelter from sun and light showers, a lightweight tarp may serve the purpose and lessen the load in your pack.

Practice erecting your tent at home before taking it on the road. Nothing is more frustrating than attempting to pitch a tent in bad weather conditions and not knowing how it is supposed to be done.

SLEEPING BAGS AND PADS

The choice of a sleeping bag will depend on the nighttime temperatures you are likely to encounter during your trip. I carried a light blanket for my first hike in the Canyon in August 1961 and a down mummy bag with a comfort rating to twenty degrees when I hiked across the Canyon in 1974. If your trip will be made during the warmer months of the year—March through September—and you plan to camp at least several thousand feet below the rim for your entire trip (no higher than Indian Garden or Cottonwood), a lightweight, compressible goose down or synthetic fill sleeping bag with a comfort range of fifty to seventy degrees Fahrenheit is advisable. You might get by with a lighter bag if you plan to sleep in a tent. If you are planning a transcanyon hike and will camp on one or both rims, a warmer bag is recommended. The nighttime temperature during the summer months can plummet into the low forties on the South Rim and the low thirties on the North Rim.

Down bags are usually lightweight, compressible, and breathable. Synthetic fill bags tend to be less expensive than down bags. Synthetic fill sleeping bags are not as compressible as down bags but retain their loft when wet, an asset when camping in rainy conditions.

A camping mattress will add immeasurably to your sleeping comfort. Considerations in choosing a camping pad include weight, bulk, comfort, insulation, and durability. There are a number of products to choose from, including air mattresses, open and closed-cell foam pads, and self-inflating pads. A camping mattress can insulate you from the cold or hot ground and protect your tired, aching body from the hard surface. I recommend choosing a pad that has a non-slip surface on at least one side—nothing is more aggravating than sliding off your pad at night. Also, pick a mattress that is resistant to punctures and tears, and, if it does become damaged, is easily reparable. Finally, size and weight must be considered. Air mattresses and long, thick, closed-cell foam pads tend to weigh more and are less compressible and take up more space in the pack. I am perfectly comfortable on a three-quarter length, self-inflating pad. It is lightweight, durable, compressible, and provides adequate insulation from the ground beneath my sleeping bag. Speaking of the ground beneath your sleeping bag—if you plan on leaving the tent at home, I recommend packing a lightweight nylon rain poncho that can double as a ground cloth to protect your sleeping bag and pad.

ILLUMINATION

Pack a headlamp, rather than a handheld flashlight. A headlamp can serve double duty as a hands-free flashlight in camp and a source of light when hiking in the dark. Make sure to pack fresh batteries before starting down the trail. LED lamps are preferable to incandescent bulb lamps. LED lamps drain batteries three to five times slower than incandescent bulbs, have a lifespan of up to 100,000 hours, and are rugged.

FIRST AID KIT

Ready-to-use first aid kits can be purchased at most pharmacies and backpacking stores and at many department stores. Unfortunately, they often contain useless items and fail to include some items I deem important; they never include medications that may be needed on a trip. I recommend creating a custom kit including an assortment of adhesive bandages, gauze pads, moleskin, adhesive tape, an elastic compression wrap, a safety pin, small tweezers to remove splinters, aspirin, nonaspirin pain reliever, an antidiarrheal medication, an antihistamine, 1 percent hydrocortisone cream for the treatment of contact dermatitis, and, depending on the length of your trip, an antibiotic. A fancy bag can be purchased to store the contents of your first aid kit but a Ziploc bag will work just as well.

REPAIR KITS AND TOOLS

1. *Pocketknife* with scissors or a multi-tool.

2. *Repair kit/maintenance tools for stove.*

3. *Repair* kit, including patches for sleeping pad.

4. Ten to fifteen feet of *nylon cord*; can be used for hanging food in camp, repairing a pack, splinting a broken bone.

5. A *small sewing kit* to repair tears in clothing and sew on buttons.

MISCELLANEOUS ITEMS

1. *Toilet paper*, if hiking in the backcountry.

2. *Small plastic sanitation trowel* for digging that all-important hole for depositing human waste.

3. *Ziploc bags* (one-quart and one-gallon size) to keep your toilet paper and matches dry and as receptacles for used toilet paper and other trash. Remember to carry out what you carried in.

4. Navigational aides; you probably won't need *topographic maps, compass or GPS receiver* when hiking the main corridor trails, but the first two items are essential when hiking in wilderness areas of the Grand Canyon.

5. *Pen or pencil, paper or a small notebook, and a camera* to record your trip in words and pictures.

6. *Toothbrush, toothpaste, and lip balm.*

7. A small plastic bottle of *biodegradable soap.*

8. A small *signal mirror* when hiking in wilderness areas.

9. An extra pair of *lightweight shoes* to wear in camp. Protect your feet at all times! Do not walk around barefoot; a foot injury could impair your ability to continue your walk. Do not walk around barefoot at night, as scorpions are out and about.

10. *Bandana*

11. *Backcountry permit* issued by the National Park Service, if you plan on camping below the rim. Obtain the Backcountry Permit Request Form online at *www.nps.gov/grca/planyourvisit/upload/permit-request.pdf.* The preferred and most competitive method for submission of a request is to fax the completed form to the Backcountry Information Center, 928-638-2125. The request can also be mailed to the Backcountry Information Center, Grand Canyon National Park, and PO Box 129, Grand Canyon, AZ 86023. E-mail requests cannot be made. A request for a permit can be made on the first of the month, four months prior to the proposed start month; for example, if an April hike is planned, apply on or after December 1. The NPS charges a $10 processing fee plus a $5 per person per night for each permit. A permit is not required for overnight stays at Phantom Ranch or dayhiking in the Grand Canyon. Each year approximately 30,000 requests are made for backcountry permits, 13,000 are issued and nearly 40,000 people camp overnight in the Canyon.

Grand Canyon Hiker's Checklist

____ Backpack with optional rain cover
____ Sleeping bag
____ Camping mattress with repair kit
____ Ground cloth/poncho
____ Tent (optional)
____ Trekking poles
____ Hiking boots/shoes, and instep crampons, if hiking during winter or early spring
____ Socks
____ Undergarments
____ Lightweight, light-colored shirt (long or short-sleeved)
____ Comfortable hiking shorts, pants, or convertible pants
____ Broad-brimmed hat
____ Lightweight sweater
____ Lightweight windbreaker
____ Bandana
____ Gloves (optional)
____ Stocking cap (optional)
____ Camp shoes or sandals (optional)
____ Water bottles/hydration system
____ Stove/fuel; repair kit for stove
____ Matches
____ Pocketknife
____ Fork and spoon
____ Cup
____ Bowl
____ Cooking pots and pans
____ Nylon scrubbing pad
____ Biodegradable soap
____ Food
____ Sunscreen
____ Lip balm
____ Sunglasses
____ Camp towel
____ Rope or cord

___ Map/compass
___ First aid kit
___ Personal hygiene items
___ Signal mirror (for backcountry use)
___ Toilet paper
___ Sanitation trowel
___ Extra plastic storage bags
___ Pen or pencil and notebook
___ Camera
___ Grand Canyon camping permit

References

1. Adkison, *Ron, Hiking Grand Canyon National Park, 2nd edition*. The Globe Pequot Press: Guilford, CT, 2006.

2. Anderson, Michael F, *Living at the Edge*. Grand Canyon Association: Grand Canyon, AZ, 1998.

3. Anderson, Michael F., editor, *A Gathering of Grand Canyon Historians, Ideas, Arguments, and First-Person Accounts*, Grand Canyon Association: Grand Canyon, AZ, 2005.

4. Berger, Todd R., *It Happened at Grand Canyon*. The Globe Pequot Press: Guilford, CT, 2007.

5. Butchart, Harvey, *Grand Canyon Treks: 12,000 Miles Through the Grand Canyon*. Spotted Dog Press: Bishop, CA, 1997.

6. Butler, Elias, and Myers, Tom, *Grand Obsession, Harvey Butchart and the Exploration of Grand Canyon*. Puma Press: Flagstaff, AZ, 2007.

7. Davis, Wade, *Grand Canyon–River at Risk*. Earth Aware Editions: San Rafael, CA, 2008.

8. Fletcher, Colin, *The Complete Walker*. Alfred A. Knoff: New York, NY, 1968.

9. Fletcher, Colin, *The Man Who Walked Through Time*. Alfred A. Knopf: New York, NY, 1968.

10. Fletcher, Colin, *River*. Alfred A. Knopf: New York, NY, 1997.

11. Ghiglieri, Michael P., and Myers, Thomas M., *Over the Edge: Death in Grand Canyon*. Puma Press: Flagstaff, AZ, 2001.

12. Henry, Marguerite, *Brighty of the Grand Canyon*. Rand McNally and Co.: Chicago, IL, 1953.

13. Hirst, Stephan, *I Am the Grand Canyon: The Story of the Havasupai People*. Grand Canyon Association: Grand Canyon, AZ, 2006.

14. Hughes, J. Donald, *In the House of Stone and Light*. Grand Canyon Natural History Association: Grand Canyon, AZ, 1978.

15. Krutch, Joseph Wood, *Grand Canyon, Today and All Its Yesterdays*. H. Wolff: New York, NY, 1957.

16. Lago, Don, *Grand Canyon Trivia*. Riverbend Publishing: Helena, MT, 2009.

17. McGarry, Susan H., *Bruce Aiken's Grand Canyon: An Intimate Affair*. Grand Canyon Association: Grand Canyon, AZ, 2007.

18. Mitchell, Stephen, translator, *Tao Te Ching*. Harper and Row: New York, NY, 1988.

19. O'Reilly, Sean, O'Reilly, James, and Habegger, Larry, editors, *Travelers' Tales: Grand Canyon*. Travelers' Tales: Palo Alto, CA, 2005.

20. Ranney, Wayne, *Carving Grand Canyon*. Grand Canyon Association: Grand Canyon, AZ, 2005.

21. Santa Fe Railroad Passenger Dept., *The Grand Canyon of Arizona.* 1909.

22. Schullery, Paul, editor, *The Grand Canyon: Early Impressions.* Pruett Publishing Co.: Boulder, CO, 1989.

23. Spangler, Sharon, *On Foot in the Grand Canyon: Hiking the Trails of the South Rim, 2nd edition.* Pruett Publishing Co.: Boulder, CO, 1989.

24. Steck, George, *Hiking Grand Canyon Loops.* Falcon: Guilford, CN, 2002.

25. Taylor, Karen L., *Grand Canyon's Long-eared Taxi.* Grand Canyon Natural History Association: Grand Canyon, AZ, 1972.

26. Thybony, Scott, *The Incredible Grand Canyon, Cliffhangers and Curiosities from America's Greatest Canyon.* Grand Canyon Association: Grand Canyon, AZ, 2007.

27. Thybony, Scott, *Official Guide to Hiking the Grand Canyon, Revised Edition.* Grand Canyon Association: Grand Canyon, AZ, 2005.

28. Thybony, Scott, *Phantom Ranch, Grand Canyon National Park.* Grand Canyon Association: Grand Canyon, AZ, 2001.

29. Thybony, Scott, *Hermit Trail.* Grand Canyon Natural History Association: Grand Canyon, AZ, 1989.

30. Wallace, Robert, *The Grand Canyon.* Time-Life Books: Chicago, IL, 1973.

31. Whitney, Stephen, *A Field Guide to the Grand Canyon, 2nd edition.* The Mountaineers: Seattle, WA, 1996.

32. Wuerther, George, *Grand Canyon: A Visitor's Companion.* Stackpole Books: Mechanicsburg, PA, 1998.